M000095312

FOOD SOURCE OF THE DAY

NATHAN WILLIAMS

©2020 All rights reserved. This book or any portion thereof may not be reproduced or used in any manner whatsoever without the express written permission of the publisher except for the use of brief quotations in a book review.

ISBN: 978-1-09830-535-2

ACKNOWLEDGMENT

Over the years I've had people challenge me and push me to be better and to push myself to do better. The one person that does this the best is my wife. When I started Brothers in Christ Outdoors, we had 30 followers after 3 years. She saw what I had going and said this was something I needed to pursue. We sent out a few friend requests and some information about what we had going and 3 years later we had around 30,000 followers and currently around 55,000 followers and reach from 1 to 2 million people per month.

I say this to say you need people around you to push you to do things that you wouldn't do. There are things that we limit ourselves to due to thinking that is all we can do and that is our limit. We place a ceiling on what we can think we can do rather than what we can really do. We are actually putting a limit on what God can do. What we need to do is take the limits off of God and see the amazing things that he can do through whatever it is that you have going. You just need to be a willing partner in the process. It is important that we realize that even though we have ideas, God placed it on our heart.

Through the journey I've had the opportunity to speak across the country and meet some amazing people along the way. I've had the opportunity to speak into others and pray for others along the way and had so many people pray for me as well. It's been a blessing to just be a part of it and to let God work through it all.

Ultimately my wife is not only my wife but she is my number 1 supporter, encourager, cheerleader, an my very best friend. I can't thank her enough for her support and her ability to push me past what I thought I could do. Thank you Cecily,

TABLE OF CONTENTS

WHERE'S YOUR FOCUS

When I first decided to take up archery, I had no idea where to start. I went and purchased a bow and a dozen arrows. I then looked into releases and broadheads. As I began to shoot and to sight my bow in I became frustrated with myself as I continued to shoot. I would shoot for hours at a time and would never be happy with the groupings I was shooting. I would sometimes shoot all twelve arrows, and most would be in a group of three inches but then a few would be scattered further out. I became obsessed with placing all 12 arrows in a three inch circle and though many would be in that circle I was never pleased with what I was accomplishing.

One afternoon I was down to my last arrow of twelve and as I focused on the target, I slowly squeezed the release and the arrow hit the mark. I had finally placed all twelve arrows in a three inch circle!!! I was on a high and I immediately wanted to do it again. The first arrow of the next group missed it by a quarter of an inch. I immediately went from a high to frustration. About that time my friend showed up and asked how I was doing. I responded to him that I had just placed all twelve arrows in the circle, and he asked why I didn't seem excited about it. I told him that the very next arrow missed the mark by a quarter of an inch. He asked me why I had taken up the sport of archery. I explained I wanted to take a deer with my bow. Then he said something that made me open my eyes to the truth of the matter. He said, "If you focus on being perfect, you're never going to enjoy it. So if you can't enjoy it then why do it?"

It took me some time to realized that the mindset that I needed to be perfect was overtaking the joy I should have been receiving from shooting my bow. I had become consumed with perfection. This same thing creeps into our new life in Christ. I see many people when they fail after salvation become frustrated and lose the joy they should have. They become consumed with perfection and if they falter a slight bit it overtakes that joy. They sometimes continue to look at what they were before and begin to think that those things of their past will destroy them. Romans 3:22-24 says, "This righteousness from God comes through faith in Jesus Christ to all who believe. There is no difference, for all have sinned and fall short of the glory of God, and are justified freely by his grace through the redemption that came by Christ Jesus." (Romans 3:22-24, New King James Version) Jesus died for our sins and we have to completely understand and receive that. We all fail, and even though we all do our best to live a life that reflects the perfection of Jesus we will still falter at times in life. What we need to do is immediately see our failures and repent and give it to God. When I say truly give it to God that means turn it over to him and let it go. God forgives us and we need to do as he has done and forgive ourselves also.

Don't beat yourself up. Understand you aren't perfect. There was only one perfect one and that was Jesus. Allow the joy of the Lord to overtake your life. Enjoy the life you've been given. Do your best to reflect Christ. God doesn't expect perfection, or he wouldn't have given his son on the cross to cover your sins. If he doesn't expect perfection in you then you shouldn't either.

Do you focus on perfection rather than progression?

Do you allow the perfection mindset get in the way of the joy you could be experiencing?

THE PURPOSE OF THE TOOL

Have you ever received something in the mail you had waited for with great anticipation? I remember the day early last year when I walked into my office and my new Athens Testament bow was laying on my desk. For us that are passionate about the sport of archery the moment your new bow is in your hand is better than Christmas morning. I couldn't wait to open the box and take hold of my new weapon of choice. As I pulled the bow out of the box, I began to admire the craftsmanship and how well made the bow was. I grabbed hold of the string and drew the bow back and I was amazed at the draw cycle and the back wall on the bow. It was smooth. I immediately took it to my buddies in the office and had to show it off. Of course, they weren't near as impressed and excited as I was. Most of these guys don't even bow hunt. When I made it home, I was showing it to my wife and explaining all that was good about the bow and I'm sure you can relate that she wasn't as nearly impressed either.

That evening I was hanging the bow up in my hunting room and realized that I needed to get on the ball and equip the bow with sights, a rest, and a stabilizer so that it could fulfill its purpose. As great as it was to hold and admire the bow that day and to show others and talk to them about archery the bows purpose wasn't for show. It wasn't a piece that is made to hang in my hunting room and make the room look better. The bow was made for a purpose and that purpose was to sling an arrow accurately at a target or wild game at 300+fps. The thing is the bow can't fulfill its purpose until it's placed in the hands of the archer.

As men we are a lot like that bow. We are all made by the hands of God. We are fearfully and wonderfully made. We are made for a purpose and we can't fulfill that purpose until we have been put in the hands of God. Proverbs 16:9 says, "The heart of man plans his way, but the Lord establishes his steps."(Proverbs 16:9, English Standard Version) We have to fully submit to Him and to allow God to tune on us and guide our direction. We have to be willing for God to correct us and help us shoot true to his calling.

Do you find yourself wondering what your purpose is? Have you been wandering through life in a seemingly aimless direction? It doesn't have to be that way. There are two groups that are having a hard time understanding their purpose. First are those who have yet to submit to God and turn their life over to him. For those of you in this group I urge you to talk to someone about a relationship with God. Find someone that has a relationship with him and is willing to speak to you. Listen to them and see how God has worked in their life. The second group are those who have given their life to Christ and are still searching for what God's plans are for them. That purpose is already inside each of you. The Holy Spirit has all the answers you need. What you must do is slow down and go to your quite place. We must do so because the Spirit has a small and still voice. With the busy life we lead and the distractions of the world it makes it difficult to hear God. I encourage you to take some time in silence this week and ask God for direction and for him to reveal your purpose. I was sitting on the back pew of a church waiting for youth service to start when God spoke to me about ministry and he has spoken to me many times sitting in a tree stand. We just need quite time with Him to find our way.

What is your purpose?

Has God put something on your heart either large or small?

Why have you no acted upon it?

TURKEY ON A TIGHT ROPE

Opening day of the 2013 turkey season was a long-awaited day. I had scouted less than I had wanted due to my busy and hectic schedule. I arrived early that morning hoping to sneak within 100 yards of a roosted gobbler and tempt him to come in with the enticing clucks and yelps of a hen. The light of a new day was starting to creep over the horizon and the gobblers began to come alive. The sound of a gobbler on a crisp spring morning is a sound everyone should hear at least once. I moved into position quickly and waited for the sound of wings as they flew down from roost.

That moment finally arrived, and the gobblers began to fly down one by one all around our property. I began to call sparingly, and the toms would sound off with each sequence of calls. They seemed to be ready to commit to come in. As I sat there for a little while I realized that all the birds were working away from me and I could hear other hens. The hens were taking the toms the other direction. My morning setup had not worked the way I was expecting.

The sun had just topped the trees and the warmth was a welcome feeling. I decided to get up and call around to see if I could find a bird that was more cooperative. I called occasionally for over an hour and decided to head back to my truck. As I walked to the southern edge of my property and called one last time a gobbler sounded off on the neighbors land adjacent to me that I had permission to hunt also. This was my last opportunity for the day so I began to sneak as close as I could before calling.

I made my way to a line of trees that lined a large open field and the tree-line the bird was in was 300 yards away. I sat my decoys in the field in front of me and began to call. The gobbler blew up with each call and began to come closer. Suddenly I saw the white head peak out of the trees and began to strut. I called occasionally just to keep him interested and he slowly made his was across the field and under two fences. Once he finally made it within gun range, I squeezed the trigger and the bird dropped in his tracks. The bird had a 10" beard, 1 1/4 in. spurs, and weighed 21 lbs.

This bird was a trophy in many people's books and the hunt was amazing with the bird strutting the entire 300 yards to my decoys. There was more than one moment that I thought for sure the bird would cluck and run away but even with his hesitation he made the fatal mistake of following the sound I was providing. He was tempted and even though I could see the tom was unsure he decided to give into that temptation. He had plenty of opportunity and time to escape.

We tend to fall into the same trap at times in our lives. Temptation is around every corner and it may feel and sound wonderful, but it can lead to death and destruction. The enemy is out to kill, steal, and destroy. 1 Corinthians 10:13 says, "No temptation has seized you except what is common to man. And God is faithful; he will not let you be tempted beyond what you can bear. But when you are tempted, he will also provide a way out so that you can stand up under it."(1 Corinthians 10:13, New International Version)

There are ways that we can be prepared to stand up under temptation. We must stay connected with God each day by getting into His word. The Bible gives us instruction and training on how to be strong under temptation. We must listen to the Holy Spirit inside each of us when he is telling us to not walk into that trap and to turn the other direction. I know that each time I've been tempted throughout my life there's been that voice telling me to not go that direction and to not give in to that temptation. We must listen to the voice. We should also surround ourselves with others to help lead, guide, and direct our path. Those should be people that will stand up and tell us when they see our footsteps are headed in the wrong direction.

Today think about the direction you're going. Are you ignoring what the Spirit is telling you? Is something inside you telling you to turn the other way? Don't be like that turkey that met his demise at the end of my barrel but be attentive to where you're going and when it doesn't seem quite right.... turn back towards the path God wants you to be on.

Are you letting temptation run your life?

What is your plan to stop the temptation from pulling you in the wrong direction?

Do you have an accountability partner to help in those situations?

SELF REFLECTION

Do you remember what it was like when you first started hunting? Do you remember all the mistakes you made and all the uncertainty in what you were doing? Recently I had a gentleman come up to me and was talking about a friend of ours that was young in his hunting career. He was telling me that on a recent hunt he had become frustrated with him due to a mistake he had made. The buck they were after had made its way in behind them as they were sitting in a ground blind. As the buck came closer to bow range the young man that is new to hunting reached to grab his bow and as he did his broadhead caught on the blind. This in turn caused the arrow to flex and bounce on his rest, making a loud noise against the riser of his bow. The buck raised his head and began stomping the ground. Moments later the buck bounced away.

As I sat and listened to my friend speak of how the other gentleman didn't know what he was doing, I began to think about how we were when we first started hunting. It took me a number of years before I took my first animal. It wasn't that I didn't have opportunities but that I was still learning through mistakes that I made along the way. I then looked back on my past and thought about the times that I had looked at the way someone else was hunting and how I was towards them. It wasn't fair of me to look at them and their mistakes and not remember that I was in the same place they were at one time.

Looking back and remembering how far we have come is important, especially in our new life in Christ. Why is it important? The first reason is to always remember where we were and how God has worked in our life. We need to never forget how in our own flesh we were weak and how far off track we truly were. In remembering we keep ourselves humble. The second reason is so that we can relate to those who are new in the faith. We must always be understanding when they fail and when they are struggling to stay on the right path. We can then help them in letting them know that we were in their shoes at one time also and that we all still have struggles in our lives. When they realize that they aren't alone it gives them a peace that they have others around them that have walked where they are at that moment in their life.

I encourage each of you to take some time today to look back and remember where you were before Christ. Then take a moment to thank God for how far he has brought you. I then encourage you to take notice of those around you that may be struggling in their new life and begin to encourage them. Explain to them that you have been where they are and that if they need someone to talk to or need help along the way that you would be glad to be there for them. I know having those people in my life that would be open and honest with me early in my walk with God was huge in my life and I know that we can all be that for others. Also, if you get the opportunity to help someone new to hunting, I encourage you to help them along the way also. It might just open a door to introduce them to Christ if they haven't taken that step yet.

Do you look back to see how far you've come in your new life in Christ?

How far have you come along the way?

Do you look for opportunities to help others grow?

BLIND SPOTS

A couple years ago I was filming for a friend of mine and we were trying to get a couple different angles of footage of the hunt. He was hurt at the time and couldn't hunt from a tree stand, so he nestled into a ground blind with another friend of ours. With two cameras rolling we were hoping to get some great footage of him harvesting a buck that he had game pics of. Our plan was to hunt until noon and then eat lunch and jump right back into the stand. As we approached late morning, we all became a little less attentive and suddenly I looked back behind his blind. The buck that he had hunted for two seasons was walking in behind him. I moved the camera around and began filming. Slowly the buck drew closer and closer and I began to zoom in as the buck moved within bow range. The buck stopped broadside at 30 yards and stood there for what seemed like minutes. My heart was pounding, and I knew at any moment I would hear the thwack of the bow letting an arrow scream towards its target. To my surprise nothing happened. He then began to slowly distance himself from the blind and slowly made his way out of sight.

I waited for ten or fifteen minutes and climbed down from the tree and walked over to the blind. My friend looked at me and asked me if everything was okay. Without saying a word, I handed him the video camera and pushed play. The look on his face was priceless when he realized the buck he was after had just slipped away. After watching the film, he realized where he had walked in and then slowly walked away. He leaned over and looked out the window of the blind. He then looked back at me and laughingly said, "That's the reason they call these things ground blinds. They have so many blind spots." He then informed me that he had positioned the blind so that he could see where he thought the deer would pass and that he never would have imagined the buck coming in from where he did. I've had this same issue while hunting from a blind. I've sat for hours, leaning and moving around to see out in every direction. Many times, I've missed or nearly missed opportunities to harvest an animal due to becoming less attentive the longer I sat and not paying attention to the blind spots.

Over the years I've realized that we can have blind spots in our life as well. Things that we become unconscious of that can hurt the relationships around us or can hurt the witness in how we walk out our life. Being oblivious to these things can make it difficult to see things in our life that can be detrimental. We can become critical of those around us and while doing so we are focused on the actions of others and at the same time paying no attention to our own actions. We can become angry with the way someone is treating us and justifying and ignoring our actions by justifying it due to theirs. We can even become blind to the fact that things such as hunting, fishing, or other hobbies are getting in the way of spending time that we should be spending with God or our families.

The truth is that we need to consistently be on guard. 1 Peter 5:8 says, "Be sober-minded; be watchful. Your adversary the devil prowls around like a roaring lion, seeking someone to devour." (1 Peter 5:8, English Standard Version) It takes us being persistent in watching for things that can get lost in the blind spots of our life. I encourage you to step back ever so often and to take a look at yourself and your actions. Ask God to help you see if any blind spots are getting in the way of what you are seeing in yourself. Also, I encourage you to develop relationships with people around you that can become accountability partners with you. Then ask them to be honest with you if they ever see anything in your life that is developing into a blind spot. Self-reflection and accountability can make a big difference in seeing the whole picture or living life with limited vision.

Do you have blind spots that are difficult for you to see in your life?

Do you have people around you that can be honest with you?

TARGET PANIC

Target panic!! It's something that every archer deals with in some form or another. We can't mistake target panic with buck fever which is caused by nervous energy causing lack of clear thinking. Target panic is when the brain seems to take over causing inaccuracy and inconsistency in your shooting. There are many different symptoms of the problem. It could be that you freeze before getting your sight on the target as if your arm has a mind of its own. You may punch your release in anticipation of your sight hitting the mark rather than holding steady on your target and allowing the release to fire by use of back tension. It could also be a number of other things.

The good thing is that we can get past the problem no matter how severe it is. How do we do this? A very helpful step in taking control of the problem is talking with others that have gone through it and allowing them to assist you. It also takes training and deprogramming the brain to fight the symptoms and we do this by hours of practice and shooting drills. One drill you can do is blind bale shooting. This is when you close your eyes and shoot blindly into a target at close range and focusing only on executing a flawless shot.

This takes part of the equation out of the process and gives you time to focus on your release alone. I actually use a resistance band and I've tied a string loop to it and as I watch tv in the living room I go through the execution of the shot. Once you get better at executing your release you can then take some time and just draw your bow and hold your sight on your mark with out firing. Doing this focuses on a different part of the shot without putting it all together. You can then later put everything together and practice, practice, practice.

As I was sitting at home doing my release drills God opened my eyes to how powerful our minds really are. I began to look at how our actions and our subconscious mind tend to lead us down the wrong path in life. These could be habits or addictions in our life that we have allowed our brain to be programmed to. It could be things such as anger, worry, etc. They could be formed through experiences of hurt from those around you. The fact of the matter is that we develop strongholds in our lives. The more we do whatever it is the more ingrained they become. The good thing is we can overcome anything and everything as long as we allow God to take control.

The first step is admitting to ourselves that we have a problem. It's not until we take that first step that we can move towards victory. 2 Corinthians 10:3-6 says, "For though we walk in the flesh, we are not waging war according to the flesh. For the weapons of our warfare are not of the flesh but have divine power to destroy strongholds. We destroy arguments and every lofty opinion raised against the knowledge of God, and take every thought captive to obey Christ, being ready to punish every disobedience, when your obedience is complete." (2 Corinthians 10:3-6, English Standard Version) We can take comfort in this scripture because even though are strongholds can be strong, God gives us the weapons to destroy them and we can destroy any influence the devil has in our life. Some of those weapons are the Word of God, prayer, praise, the name of Jesus, the power of the Holy Spirit, the gifts of the spirit, and our testimonies. The power of God is greater than anything the devil can throw our way. We just have to tap into the weaponry that God has supplied.

What I want you to do is to take a step back and open your eyes to things that may be strongholds in your life. Are there things that you are doing out of hurt or addiction? Are your actions being affected negatively by the way your mind has been programmed by the enemy? Take that first step and be honest with yourself. Once you've done this, I encourage you to take some time in prayer asking God to begin a transformation of your mind. Begin to take each thought and action captive and allow God to transform the way you go about things. God has given each of us the weapons to destroy the strongholds in our lives. We just have to learn how to use them. I also encourage you to seek out someone to talk to or send us a message. Also, we must always remember the Philippians 4:13 that says, "I can do all things through Him who gives me strength." (Philippians 4:13, New International Version)

What strongholds do you deal with in your life?

Are they from insecurities or from past hurts and pains?

What is the best way to deal with these?

CONSISTENCY COUNTS

Over the years I've learned that one of the biggest things in archery is consistency. Years ago, I would pick my bow up a month before season and once the archery season was over it would go back in the bow case until the following season drew near. Needless to say I struggled to stay consistent with my shooting and missed opportunities in the early bow seasons to fill the freezer. These days I've learned to be more consistent in shooting throughout the entire year to be able to shoot well. The thing is, you may be shooting often and there could still be things that you aren't doing repetitively as you should. Not only do you have to be consistent in practicing, you must focus on form, anchor point, working your release, bow maintenance, and so many other things that if you are inconsistent then you will struggle to shoot accurately.

This parallels our spiritual life in that if we aren't consistently seeking God then we will easily get off track and it will be difficult to follow his direction. It's extremely easy for a man in this world to veer towards the ways of the world due to momentary pleasures. It takes dedication and focus to move forward in God's plans for you.

The consistency also goes for disciplines in our walk like staying in the Word, fellowship with other believers, serving others, and much more.

I encourage you to take a look at your life. Are you being consistent in prayer with God, studying his word, fellowship? Are you dedicated to grow with God each day? Could you do better and do you want to draw closer in your relationship with our heavenly Father? It takes dedication and consistency. Make it a point to make time for daily prayer and studying of the Word. If it takes waking up 30 minutes earlier to do so I suggest you take that opportunity to allow the Father to fill you up first thing in the morning so that his love can overflow through you as you go through your day. Be proactive in fellowship with other believers. If you don't have a church, then find one and if you can find a men's our couples small group I encourage you to do so. We grow by building each other up and helping each other move forward. Look for areas to serve and reflect Jesus in your community and your home. There are ways to serve around every corner. Be consistent. Be dedicated. Grow with Jesus. Together let's change this world.

Where can you become more consistent in your daily walk?

What do you plan on changing to get that consistency?

LOSING YOUR PEACE

Over the past few years I've gotten much better about not letting things that don't truly matter in life get to me. Years ago, I lost a bass that at that point in time would have more than likely been the new Oklahoma state record. That afternoon I was disappointed to the point I literally became sick. When hunting I've missed out on opportunities to harvest the buck I've been after due to poor decision on where or when to hunt. I followed that with beating myself up and getting down from the situation. This didn't happen just in my outdoor life. When watching the Oklahoma Sooner games, I would get upset when they weren't playing well and let that affect my attitude. Don't get me wrong I still fall in this area at times in my life, but I have continually grown.

Over time I've learned to take a step back when I begin to get this way. I then ask myself one question. "Is it worth losing your peace over?" That's a pretty simple question and more than likely the answer to the question is "not at all". We all become passionate about certain things. We all become completely caught up in certain moments that we feel should have had a different outcome. The thing is most of those things don't truly matter in our life at all. In fact, those things that we tend to get upset about are actually getting in the way of our daily walk and our relationship with God. It could be at your work and the failure to receive a promotion. God has provided for you your entire life. He isn't going to stop now. It could be a football game that you feel was stolen by a bad call. In all actuality somewhere throughout that season the shoe has been on the other foot and your team was probably given a game due to a bad call. The truth is these guys are paid millions of dollars to play a game and what happens in a game really can't have a positive outcome on your life. It can have a negative outcome by robbing you of the peace God has given you though. It could be that you've been completely consumed of wanting to harvest a certain trophy buck and when you find out the person across the road has been blessed with the harvest you become discouraged. You must realize that there are many other deer growing up to have the same potential that buck had and there is always hope to harvest one of those in the future.

This brings me to something Charles Spurgeon once said. "God will empty out all that thou hast before He will put His own into thee; He will first clean out thy granaries before He will fill them with the finest of the wheat. The river of God is full of water; but not one drop of it flows from earthly springs. God will have no strength used in His battles but the strength which He Himself imparts. Are you mourning over your own weakness? Take courage, for there must be a consciousness of weakness before the Lord will give thee victory. Your emptiness is but the preparation for your being filled, and your casting down is but the making ready for your lifting up." These words are profound. Are you weak in certain area? Is it hard to admit your weakness? We must be conscious of our weakness before the Lord and claim victory over them. We must empty ourselves of earthly things such as pride and anger so that the Lord can fill us with things such as humbleness and joy. Drop the walls you've built up around yourself so that God can then lift you up to victory.

I want to challenge you to do one thing today. When you begin to get upset over something ask yourself this question. "Is this enough to lose my peace over?" Don't let emotions answer that question. Give yourself the honest answer.

Do things of this words rob you of your peace easily?

Do those things truly matter in life?

ROUGH WEATHER DEVOTION

It's 4 a.m. and I crawl out of bed. I stumble into the living room and take a peek outside. It's cold. It's very cold and the wind is howling. I think for a second to crawl back into the bed, but I think about the beauty of a mallard committing to my decoy spread. I grab my gear and begin to dress and grab my things and head out the door. I arrive to my destination soon after and begin to set out my decoys. It's still cold and my face and hands are already numb. The wind is blowing harder and harder and there is moisture in the air. As the sun begins to shine the light into this world the first mallards begin to commit, and I hear the blast of success off in the distance. I begin to call and suddenly my first eager mallard begins to move my direction. He circles, legs down, wings cupped, he begins his ascent. I wait for the perfect moment and squeeze the trigger. The sound resonates from my barrel, the shot screams through the air, then suddenly the first bird of the year is down. The adrenaline rush is warming, and I have quickly lost the realization that my face and hands were freezing moments earlier.

As hunters and fishermen, we've all experienced something like this. The amazing gift that God has given us in harvesting whatever we are pursuing. The adrenaline rush that seems to take over and wipe out whatever discomfort we were facing before. As I looked back on the hunt I was describing, one thing really came to mind. That one thing is devotion. I could have easily crawled back into bed that morning and slept in, but I was devoted to the passion God has put in my heart. If it weren't for that devotion, I would have never experienced the gift God put in front of me in that beautiful green head.

Being devoted to something is key in being successful and growing in whatever, it is you are pursuing. This holds true especially in your walk with the Lord. Acts 2:42 says, "All the believers DEVOTED THEMSELVES to the apostles teaching, and to fellowship, and to sharing in meals (including the Lord's Supper), and to prayer."(Acts 2:42, New Living Translation) One thing in this scripture that really stands out is the word "ALL". Can you imagine if every believer fully devoted themselves to the Lord each day. This world would change drastically. The truth is our spiritual growth is dependent on our devotion. It is OUR responsibility individually. Your pastor can't lead you enough, your spouse can't love you enough, and your friends can't do enough to make you grow. They can all help but can't do it for you. Your growth and success, or failure, is ultimately on YOU. God loves you and wants a relationship with you. It's going to take one thing from you to have that relationship grow and that is for you to be devoted to that relationship. It's not always going to be easy, but it will be worth it.

Today I want you to stop and reflect on a couple of things. Take a look, at what you are devoted to. Are you devoted to hunting? Do you endure tough circumstances yet push on towards the goal? Do you give up things to pursue a trophy whitetail or whatever game you pursue? What are you devoted to in your life? Now ask yourself the most important questions. Are you fully devoted to the Lord? When things get tough do you push forward acknowledging God is by your side? Do you let the world and things of this world that will fade away get in the way of your devotion needed to grow? Are you doing everything you can to focus on God each day? Are you allowing God to lead you or are you following the world? Take some time to reflect on your life and honestly answer the question, "Am I fully devoted to God?". Once you answer that question truthfully you will know what direction you need to go. I would encourage you to devote yourself to that direction.

Do you find yourself fully devoted to God as you are the hunting or whatever it is you pursue?

What does devotion mean to you?

CALL SHY

The morning was still and quiet. The wind had laid overnight and the crisp cool was in the air. My son and I slowly slipped deep into the timber hoping to get close to a long beard as he came down from his roost. The sun was slowly beginning to lighten the eastern sky and the fog was sifting through the trees. Suddenly the quite peace of the morning was shattered by the sound of an old gobbler. Then another sounded off in the far distance. We began to set a plan into motion and slipped within 70 yards of the roost. Knowing that we were hunting public land and the birds were extremely call shy we decided to only do a fly down call. Suddenly we heard the flapping of wings as they descended from their perch. I made a couple of cluck and purrs and laid the call down. The silence was deafening as we waited. Suddenly the gobbler blew up once more and we realized he went the opposite direction.

My son looked at me and said, "Oh well, that was awesome any-way." We grabbed our things and decided to head back towards the truck since we only had a short window to hunt before church. As we made our way around a field I glanced across the fence and noticed a gobbler feeding away from us. My son crawled into position and I pulled out my slate call. As I watched the gobbler be oblivious to our location, I yelped at him and as I did I noticed the bird immediately ran the opposite direction. The morning hunt was over and we went home empty handed.

As I drove home, I was thinking of ways I could have changed the situation and helped my son harvest his bird. Knowing that the birds we were hunting had been pressured aggressively being that it was public land we decided to be more gentle and build the birds curiosity rather than do a lot of calling. The more I thought of it I realized that no matter what I did with that bird I would have had a hard time calling him in. More than likely I would have had to of known where that bird was going and set up waiting for him to show up.

The more I thought on the situation I also began to think about how difficult it is at times to draw someone to Christ. Many times, the person God has placed on our heart is somewhat call shy. They could have been pressured by someone in their past or they could have been busted by someone that wasn't being careful in the situation they were in. Either way it makes it difficult to get that person to answer the call and many times we give up on that person. The truth is that the rejoicing in heaven when anyone gives their life to Christ is grand and we need to understand how great that truly is. Luke 15:7 says "I say to you that likewise there will be more joy in heaven over one sinner who repents than over ninety-nine just persons who need no repentance." (Luke 15:7, King James Version)

So how do we move forward when it becomes difficult for someone to let go of self and let God have control? The first thing we need to realize is that persistence usually pays off in the end. We can't stop pursuing them because God never stops pursuing us. We then have to always allow his light shine through us in our daily life and we must continually approach the person with love and compassion. We all have struggles and being transparent with them and letting them know that we struggle also helps tremendously.

I encourage you today that if you've been pursuing someone for Christ, please don't give up. Be persistent and build that relationship in a way that Jesus would through love. Reflect him in your actions with that person. If one method isn't working, then change up the call a little and if it doesn't work today that doesn't mean that it won't work tomorrow. Go out and continue to call and in the right time the heavens will be rejoicing loudly for the newest child of God has arrived!

When approaching someone that may have been hurt in the past or is hard to approach due to misconceived thoughts, what is the best way to do so?

What is most important when reaching other? Facts or relationship?

FOCUSED ATTENTION

As turkey hunters we all know that magical moment as the sun is beginning to shine light upon the day and off in the distance the sound of a gobble echoing through the trees. I remember my first time hearing that glorious sound. I had waited for that moment for some time. I jumped out of bed early that morning and was in the woods for what seemed like an eternity before daylight. I stood motionless, leaned up against a massive oak tree where I saw birds the past deer season. I pulled my hoot owl call from my bag and gave it a shot of air. Without much hesitation a short distance away a gobbler shouted back. My heart nearly jumped out my chest. I dropped to the ground and set up my ground blind and positioned myself with shotgun rested on my knee. It was only a few minutes later when I heard the sound of wings and the crashing of leaves. I let out a few yelps and became quite once again. My decoys were moving slightly in the morning breeze and as I watch them, I suddenly see movement coming up the ridge. My nerves were becoming shaky and I realized it was a hen. She moved towards the decoys and everything was just right when I noticed the fan of a gobbler creeping up behind her. The tom came in showing all his colors. His head changed from white, to red, and to blue. His fan was full and perfect. As I watched the tom courting the hen and paying full attention to her I looked for an opportunity to take my shot. He made his way around the decoys and I slowly squeezed the trigger. The bird was down and I had been successful in harvesting my first bird.

As I sat and ran this experience through my mind this morning, I continually thought about the time the tom was courting the hen. He was fully attentive to her and she was the most important thing to him at the moment. He blew up in size as his feathers stood on end. His fan was on full display with his head tucked into his body. He was doing everything he could do to win her over. If time and my shotgun would have allowed the tom more than likely would have been successful in winning over the breeding rights to this hen. Once he had been successful, he would have moved on and lost interest in this one that he had been so attentive and longing after.

As men I see us do this very same thing in our relationships. When we first have the opportunity to court a woman that has caught our interest, we do everything possible to win this woman over. We lose sleep, we go out of the way, and we even do things that we wouldn't tell our buddies about. I remember many hour long drives to and from my wife's apartment for the opportunity to spend even the shortest amount of time with her. I once took my lunch hour and drove 30 miles to take some fruity candy to her at her work. I didn't know exactly which fruity candy she liked so I took four different kinds just to make sure I got one that she would love.

The thing is we often times fail to continue this same type of attention and affection for our spouse as time begins to float by. We both
become content and comfortable in our relationship. We have already
won the other person over so why continue to make that same effort.
The truth is that our relationship with our spouse should reflect the
relationship of Christ and the church. Ephesians 5:25, "Husbands,
love your wives, as Christ loved the church and gave himself up for
her," (Ephesians 5:25, New International Version) This is pretty clear
that we should show continual love, attention, and affection towards
our spouse since Christ is unchanging in pursuing us. I've heard men
say that it's hard because their wife has also become comfortable and
life has made everything so busy that she has failed to show him that
same affection and attention. This is no different than her being the
church, or the people being the church, towards Christ. I see people
all the time become comfortable in their relationship with God and
become stagnant in their longing and attention towards him. The
amazing thing is that God never becomes stagnant towards us. His
love is everlasting and unconditional. He is consistently pursuing us
and he is consistently showing us the love he has for us.

As men it's our responsibility in our relationships to continually
pursue and love our wives. We should always come in like that tom
turkey in full strut and showing her our affection and our intent on
winning her over each day. It doesn't matter what her reaction is just
like in the relationship with us and God. It's our duty and our blessing to be able to reflect Christ in the consistent pursuit and affection
towards our spouse. Trust me when I say that over time the love and
affection will begin to flow back in your direction.

Do you still pursue your wife your wife in the same way you did when you were courting her?

What makes you pursue her less or more today?

How do you plan to change this for the better?

INTENTIONAL WAYS

As I sit here this morning, I'm looking forward to getting back in the tree stand before season is over. We have 7 days left to hunt and with the bucks out looking for food I'm hoping the urge to fill one's belly brings him across my path. When I get like this I start thinking and setting my game plan for the upcoming hunt. I look at the temperature and the wind. I then decide where I'm going to hunt. I have my route to enter that stand already laid out so not to spook anything in the area. I am intentional on every part of the hunt.

As I thought about this I was convicted to a point. When it came to me thinking about my hunt, I was noticing how intentional I was in all aspects of that hunt. What I realized is that I was failing to be intentional in a much more important part of my life. I was looking forward to the hunt and I was living with expectation that I would have an encounter with a buck of a lifetime. I knew that once I climbed up in the tree, I would be watchful for that trophy buck. I would be looking for even the slightest movement in the brush and I would be on high alert the entire time.

What I was failing to do is be on alert for opportunities throughout my day ahead of me to reach someone who is needing Christ in their life. I realized that I was failing to be intentional on keeping my eyes open for the slightest need in someone's life. So many people out there need to experience the love of Christ through each of us. We are his vessels here in this world and we need to capitalize on those opportunities that we so often miss throughout the day. Why do we miss them? It could be our busy lives, worldly priorities, and it could even be distractions such as looking forward to a hunt. I never want to miss an opportunity to be the messenger from God to help save someone's life. I encourage each of you today to start your day off in prayer and make it a point to be intentional in seeing the world around you. See it through the eyes of God and be bold in reaching out and loving on someone. I understand that it can be difficult at times to be that bold, but I can promise you one thing. God is right beside you. Deuteronomy 31:6 says, "Be strong and courageous. Do not be afraid or terrified because of them, for the LORD your God goes with you; he will never leave you nor forsake you."(Deuteronomy31:6, New International Version)

Do you get so caught up in your own day to day to see what is going on around you?

Do you try to see what is going on around you throughout the day to see opportunities to speak into the life of other?

What scares you to reach out to start a conversation with someone about something they may be going through?

EXPERIENCE MATTERS

I sit here remembering when I first went deer hunting with my dad. He had been going through chemo treatments and I was just kind of learning on my own how to actually hunt. I had asked dad if he wanted to go hunting the following morning and he initially said no but later called and said he would go.

The following morning, we arrived a little late mainly because I was young and didn't really know how to get to my stand. We rolled in about 30 minutes after daylight and I headed off to where I had found some good rubs. Dad asked me where I was going and suggested I go over by the west fence. I looked at him as if I was a seasoned pro and said I knew where I was going to sit.

Dad walked towards the west fence and just as I settled into my spot, I heard a gunshot ring. I couldn't tell if it was dad, or someone else so I sat tight. About 30 minutes later I heard 2 other shots and I was pretty sure they came from the muzzle of dad's gun so I slowly made my way to the west fence and found him in his blue jeans, red jacket, and his vest. As I approached him, I noticed he was looking on the ground for a blood trail. I had seen nothing, and he was looking for blood.

I'm going to stop there and give you the rest of the story in another post but for this post I want to point out that I was a fool. Dad had tried to give me good advice and I was too hard-headed to listen. I mean I had been scouting and he hadn't even been in the woods. Little did I know that the knowledge in his head outweighed my scouting by a long shot.

This brings me to Proverbs 12:15 which says, "The way of fools seems right to them, but the wise listen to advice." (Proverbs 12:15, New International Version) So many times in life I'm guilty of having something stuck in my head and not willing to listen to others around me. My mindset is that they can't know more than me on the subject. It's been on my mind and they've not even been thinking about it so that makes me the expert right? Wrong!

So many times, we think we know the answer and we know the right direction to go yet we really are clueless. It's a good thing that God places people in our paths like our dads, our friends, and especially our spouses to help keep us on the right track and it's important that we humble ourselves to receive from those people. Now we aren't always right or wrong and the same goes with the other party, but God is always right. We need to be a people that comes together and takes things to God for direction on matters in our lives. In the instance that neither are hearing exactly what to do it's important to have others around you that you can go to. Proverbs 11:14 says

"Where there is no guidance, a people falls, but in an abundance of counselors there is safety." (Proverbs 11:14, English Standard Version)

I encourage you today to listen to those around you. Your dad knows a lot. Your friends see things from a different perspective. Your spouse has your well-being in mind in being one with you and when you make it a habit to be intentional in your communication with your partner it can open up a network between the two of you that becomes filled with trust and compassion. Build a group of people that you can go to and come together in prayer on things that are going on in your life. Do these things intentionally so that when things do start moving in your life, it will run a lot smoother for everyone.

Are you guilty of thinking you had all the answers?

Have you ignored good advice to find out later you should have listened?

KEEP THE GAME PLAN

As hunters we work extremely hard to pursue the buck that we are after each year. Some of us name them and even build a hit list of animals we plan to test our wits against each season. Sometimes we are successful but many times we don't see the harvest of that animal come to fruition.

So how do we begin to turn the tide on seeing our hard work pay off more often? The answer lies within the way we think. It comes from our perspective. The best way to put the animal you're pursuing in your path is to begin to think like the deer himself. We have to open our minds to what that deer needs and how he sees the habitat he resides in. One way we can do this is to see it from a higher level by looking at topographical maps and begin to ask ourselves a few questions. Where is the best bedding area? What are his food sources? Where are the easiest, yet safest, travel corridors for that buck to travel to and from those areas? When we begin to see those things and begin to eliminate certain areas we can then begin to put a game plan into action and up our chances of harvesting that animal.

Many times, the key is to stick to the game plan no matter what. I've missed opportunities a few times at the buck I was pursuing by chasing rubs or scrapes I've seen as I was easing in or out of my stand location. I've set up on a rub line or a scrape during the pre-rut in hopes the deer would show his face and as I look at the game cam, a few days later he was making his way to feed just before dark on the trail I had determined was his path from bed to dinner while I had become distracted by the rub or scrape.

As I was sitting here thinking on how a deer would think, and experiences in the past, it brought me to my mindset as it pertains to my walk with God. Our goal is that our daily walk will be reflective of Jesus Christ himself. So how do we do that? The answer lies in our perspective. We have to begin to see life from a higher level, or a heavenly perspective.

Isaiah 55:8-9 says, "For my thoughts are not your thoughts, neither are your ways my ways," declares the Lord. As the heavens are higher than the earth, so are my ways higher than your ways and my thoughts than your thoughts." (Isaiah 55:8-9, New International Version) Our thoughts and our ways are many times skewed by what's going on in our life at the present time. We lose the big picture while we are chasing what's going on at that moment in our life. We tend to see what's right in front of our face, and we lose the big picture at times. It could be problems we are facing, our jobs, running kids here and there, or it could even be the ministry we are doing at the time.

The truth is those things need to be handled but we can't let those things distract us away from the higher perspective that we need to be seeing life from. If we keep focused and see life from God's eyes we then begin to see the things we could have missed if we were focused only on what was right in front of our face. Things such as a friend needing someone to talk to, your wife needing prayer, your kids needing attention and guidance, or even God giving you direction in your life.

I encourage you today to turn your focus back to a heavenly perspective. Begin to see everything from a higher level. When you do this, problems won't look as big and overwhelming, you will see those around you better, and you will begin to see the needs surrounding your daily life. Begin to see life through the eyes of our Father in heaven.

Do you see things from a heavenly perspective?

Do you tend to stick to the plan?

ACTIONS VS INTENTIONS

Have you ever heard the saying, "We tend to judge others by their actions, and we judge ourselves by our intCentions."? We see this in our own lives and in the lives of those around us. I was speaking to a friend a few weeks ago that was condemning a neighbor of his for shooting a buck that my friend considered a future trophy. He was extremely frustrated and speaking negatively about the man who harvested the deer. The deer was a 4 year old 10 point that scored approximately 125 inches. This caught my attention because my friend had harvested a 3 year old 8 point that would have scored around 110 inches just a week before we were having this conversation. I asked him what the difference was in his harvest and the other mans harvest and his response was that he decided to take the 8 point as a management buck. He then went on to say the neighbor was one that would shoot anything that walks by. Being that I knew both people I knew the intentions of both. My friend I was speaking to was honest in the fact he shot the 8 point to help manage the herd in the area. The man my friend was speaking of was also a man I know very well. This man's intentions weren't on management but on filling his freezer. Not only had he already harvested a doe, but I know that he had already passed up the 8 point my friend had harvested. This was also the largest buck this man had ever harvested in his 25 years of hunting.

As I've lived my life, I've noticed how often we criticize others and how quick we are to judge them. At the same time, we make excuses for things we do in our life and point out that our intentions were in the right place. The truth is, we cannot rightly judge anyone else, because we do not know the contents of their heart. We all make mistakes in life.

This also holds true when we look at the lives of fellow Christians around us. There have been many times that I've stepped out to serve the Lord that didn't quite work the way I wanted. I remember the first time that I spoke to a group and I heard criticism from a few people in the following days. To be honest, my entire life I had always been very reserved and would have never stepped up in front of anyone to speak. I give the good Lord praise that I have finally overcome that and have been able to do just that. I hear people talking in passing about how they didn't like the sermon, music, prayer, or some other part of the service. We almost grade those around us and in doing so we have a critical spirit. Romans 14:10 says, "Why do you criticize and pass judgment on your brother? Or you, why do you look down upon or despise your brother? For we shall all stand before the judgment seat of God. And so each of us shall give an account of himself - give an answer in reference to judgment - to God. Then let us no more criticize and blame and pass judgment on one another, but rather decide and endeavor never to put a stumbling block or an obstacle or a hindrance in the way of a brother." (Romans 14:10-13, Amplified) wether it be immaturity, negativity, the devil, or insecurity, we need to make it a point to get past this so that we can further the kingdom of God. So how do we do this? First and foremost we need to focus on ourselves and our betterment before looking at those around us. Matthew 7:3 says, "Why do you look at the speck of sawdust in your brother's eye and pay no attention to the plank in your own eye?" (Mathew 7:3, New International Version) If we spend more time on bettering ourselves individually then we will grow stronger together. The second thing we need to do is build those around us up rather than tearing them down. 1 Thessalonians 5:11 says, "Therefore encourage one another and build one another up, just as you are doing." (1 Thessalonians 5:11, English Standard Version) The people around you need to hear words of encouragement. When they fail they need to have your support so that they can have the confidence to give it another shot. When people feel as if they have others on their side, they become stronger and in turn become more motivated to become better themselves.

In encourage you today to focus on two things. Look at yourself and your life rather than judging those around you. Be intentional and honest with yourself so that you can better reflect Jesus. Also ask yourself if you've been critical of those around you and make a concsious effort to speak encouragement to them. Understand that when they are trying to do things, they are more than likely doing it with good intent. Be their support system.

*Do you find yourself judging other by how you would
do things?*

*Is it fair to say the way you do things is the best way
for everyone?*

UNEXPECTED VOICE

This evening as I sat patiently waiting for a deer to show, I kept reading scripture and praying to God. He has continued to give me words to put down and share with others through devotionals or just words of encouragement. Tonight was different. As I sat there nothing was coming to mind. I finally kicked back and enjoyed the evening. A woodpecker lighted on a tree a few feet away. A squirrel scurried up a tree and soared limb to limb as he made his way to his den. As the glow of the sun disappeared, I gathered my bow and climbed down from the stand.

As I proceeded to make my way down the ridge, across a grassy hill and eventually to a trail that led back to my truck I heard God speak. This was only my fifth time I have been able to get into the woods this year and I was successful at harvesting a deer 3 of the first 4 hunts. I was hoping to go 4 for 5 but that wasn't the case. In my mind I had just about called this an unsuccessful hunt until I heard these words. "The deer didn't show up but I did."

Wow! Yes, you did God! You never fail and you are omnipresent. Thank you, God.

In life we tend to call things unsuccessful when they don't go the way we think they should have gone. In fact, we get frustrated at those situations quite often. The truth is, if we would listen God is trying to communicate with us that no matter how we think things should go, he has our best interest at heart and he is Emanuel "God with us" and this goes for those times that we may think he is nowhere around.

Joshua 1:9 says "Have I not commanded you? Be strong and courageous. Do not be frightened, and do not be dismayed, for the Lord your God is with you wherever you go." (Joshua 1:9 New International Version) I want to focus on the dismayed part of this scripture. Dismayed means sudden loss of courage or resolution or sudden disappointment. So many times in life things happen different than what we had in mind and we are disappointed in the outcome because we are focused on self rather than what God wants or has in store for us. I can assure you that what God has is better than anything we can dream. If we consistently stay in communication with Him, we will be able to understand and handle these things in a higher light and heavenly understanding.

I want to encourage you to stay in communion with God and to trust Him in an irrational way. Walk in an immeasurable faith that God is with you. Walk in a faith that is infectious to those around you.

Oh and by the way, on those hunts that I don't kill a deer, God usually has the ability to give me the spiritual nourishment that I need that is so much more beneficial than the physical nourishment he provides in venison. So... every hunt is a successful one!!!

Have you been discouraged by focusing on what you expected?

What should you have focused om during that time?

DISTRACTIONS IN THE AIR

Opening day has finally arrived. The alarm blasts through the air even though I've been awake in anticipation of this moment. I ease out of bed and stumble through the house trying to not wake the family. I slip my camo on and gather my gear as I go through a mental checklist.... bow, arrows, release, cover scent, flashlight, etc. I have everything and head out the door.

After the short drive to my property I spray down and grab my gear. With every step in the red glow of my light I slowly and carefully ease through the timber in hopes I don't cause a deer to send a resounding blast of warning throughout the woods. As I arrive to my stand, I take a deep breath that I made it unscathed.

It's 6am. One hour before daylight. The woods are motionless and without sound. My breath and the ever so slight thumping of my heart is all I can hear. I listen intently in hopes of hearing the buck I passed last year and praying he is bigger than he was eleven months ago.

It's 6:30 and off in the distance I hear the rustling of leaves. As it draws closer, I hear more rustling deeper in the woods to my left. I think to myself that this has to be deer and my heart begins to race.

It's 6:45 and the woods have become quite once again. I begin to second guess what I believed were deer moments before. Suddenly from the pasture at the bottom of the ridge a cow bellows and breaking the silence. Moments later a pack of coyotes begin to howl just behind me sending chills throughout the air. The thunderous wings of an owl shakes the tree as it lands in the limb above me. The wind begins to blow and the leaves rustle as the birds begin to fill the air with song. It's a beautiful thing to experience.

As I turn to look in front of me, I notice that the Lord has provided the light I needed to see the deer I had given up on moments earlier. The problem was that she had just walked two steps past my shooting lane. I grabbed my bow and moved into position in hopes she would turn around and give me the shot I had wanted. Suddenly she walked away and disappeared as quickly as she had appeared.

As God was speaking to me through this situation, he showed me that we seem to get distracted and pulled off course rather easily. Many of those things look and sound nice buy many times they aren't good for our relationship with God. For many of us God has given us a dream or vision of something, but we have allowed things of this world to pull our attention away from Him and whatever it is he has shown us.

Isaiah 26:3-4 says, "People with their minds set on you, you keep completely whole, Steady on their feet, because they keep at it and don't quit. Depend on God and keep at it because in the Lord God you have a sure thing."(Isaiah 26:3-4, The Message Bible) In this world we only have one sure thing and that's our Father in heaven. We can rest assured that his unconditional love for us and those around us will never fail.

So where do our problems begin? It's when we have our minds set on things of this world and we begin to live within ourselves and not the father that we begin to stumble and become unsteady. We forget about the direction he was taking us and begin to make our own way. As we all know that path leads to destruction and failure.

I encourage you today to set all distractions aside and come back to the Father. Be still and know that he is God. Listen to Him and allow Him to lead you. Surrender to Him. No matter how great you think the path your making is, the Father's is even greater. Set your mind on him to be completely whole and steady. Don't quit and depend on the only sure thing.

Do you get easily distracted by other things around you?

Do you focus on the things that truly matter?

ARROWS OF FIRE

What comes to your mind when you think of an outdoorsman? For me it's always been a positive thought for the most part. These are a few things that have always come to my mind. Courteous, patient, caring, good steward, fair, hard working, driven, and I could go on but for the sake of making this post to long I'll stop there. Honestly, I've always been proud of outdoorsmen at large in the way they carry themselves and what they stand for.

Over the last few days it's really disturbed me on how many of our fellow outdoorsmen and hunters have acted over the mistake over Carbon Express arrows on Walmart's website. I've read countless posts of fellow hunters berating managers and employees at the sporting goods counter so they can get the dozen arrows for the price of one. I agree that Walmart had them priced incorrectly on their website but what bothers me is how people reacted and treated those they came in contact with, just to get free arrows at the cost of someone's mistake. That mistake was made by one person in an office somewhere in Walmart's corporate offices. A simple mistake that could have happened to anyone, including myself. That manager, sporting goods worker, or the person at the register had nothing to do with the mistake other than doing their job.

I want to shed light on a few things that are more important than getting a few arrows for free. Scripture says in Luke, "Do to others as you would have them do to you." (Matthew 7:12, New International Version) I want to ask you something. If you owned a business and let's say you made a mistake on pricing that would lose your company a lot of money, how would you want those you deal with to react and to treat you. Me personally I would want them to treat me fairly and allow me to sell whatever it may be at a fair price. In the businesses that my wife and I own it would hurt us tremendously if we were to make a mistake such as the one over the arrows.

Moving on from there I've read many posts saying that Walmart has plenty of money that they can handle the loss for our gain. Honestly this is true, but is it the way we should do business with anyone? Leviticus 25:14 "And if you make a sale to your neighbor or buy from your neighbor, you shall not wrong one another."(Leviticus 25:14, English Standard Version) The truth is, the price was wrong and everyone who went to attack those employees who had no part of the mistake knew the price was wrong and it was a mistake. In turn they knew that it wasn't a fair transaction. It doesn't matter if we are dealing with a multi-billion dollar corporation, brick and mortar store on main street, or a vendor on the street somewhere, we should always deal with everyone in a fair manner.

Last but by far not the least I want to address Jesus in this situation. 1 John 2:6 says "Whoever says he abides in him ought to walk in the same way in which he walked."(1 John 2:6, English Standard Version) Our goal in life is for our walk to resemble the walk of Jesus Christ. So, if that's the case and we all want to resemble Jesus I want us all to put ourselves in this situation. Put yourself in the place of the person who made the minor mistake of pricing the arrows incorrectly. Let's say an individual who claims to be Christian comes to purchase those arrows comes and begins to berate that person because of their mistake. How do you think that person is going to relate to Jesus? How do you think the other people in the store who are seeing the reaction over some arrows are going to relate that to Jesus? To be honest they won't see Jesus at all in that situation and in turn we fail to allow God to shine through in that moment.

In closing I want to leave you with these few things. Those people working behind the counter and in store management didn't make the mistake in pricing. They do not deserve to be treated poorly due to that mistake. That person who entered the price incorrectly is only human and are prone to mistakes just like we are. As hunters and outdoorsmen, the way we act and react in these situations is a reflection of who we are. It can be a positive or a negative reflection and how those around us perceive it can be a powerful thing. This not only pertains to us as outdoorsmen but more importantly as Christians. If you claim to be a Christian you should do everything in your power to show that in the way you act, treat others, and how you go about your walk daily. Situations like this can be detrimental in turning someone to Christ. James 4:1 says, "What causes quarrels and what causes fights among you? Is it not this, that your passions are at war within you?"(James 4:1, English Standard Version) I'll leave you with this question. Is the passion of hunting or money more important than the people we come in contact with? I'm thankful that I have a God that shows mercy and grace in spite of my mistakes. I can only hope I show the same to those around me.

Are you one to try to take advantage of a situation caused by the mistake of someone else?

Is that situation more important than the person you are dealing with?

How can something like this be a positive or negative thing?

A LIGHT IN THE DARKNESS

Over the last week we've been in L.A. ministering on the streets to many amazing people. There are around 44,000 people who sleep outside each night in L.A. and as we ministered on Skid Row it brought the life we have into perspective. Each evening the team would gather up and we would share our highs and lows for the day and minister to one another. As we visited with some of the team throughout the week they were feeling as if they could have done more.

On Friday morning as I was sitting in the chapel before starting our day God brought me back an experience I had a few years back. I was hunting public land and after scouting for weeks I had found a bend in the creek where there was a good deer crossing. This particular morning I parked my truck, grabbed my bow and climbing stand, then realized my flashlight batteries were nearly dead. My stand location was nearly 3/4 of a mile from the main road but I thought the light would last until I made my way in. Unfortunately, they only lasted about half a mile and due to me trying to get in my stand an hour before daylight I was still a quarter mile from the creek with no light to guide me. The morning was cloudy and with there being no moon, it would have been difficult to find my way in the dark. After a few moments I decided to hunt that morning where I was standing so I grabbed my climber and eased up in a nearby tree.

As I got comfortable in the stand I looked around and had no idea what my surroundings were like. No matter how hard I looked I could see nothing. After a few minutes I noticed a faint glow in the distance coming through the brush. As it drew near I realized it was another hunter. He came closer and closer and ended up walking directly under my stand and as his light passed, I caught a glimpse of my surroundings. Soon he was out of sight but what I noticed was after the light passed and my mind caught a glimpse of what was around me I began to see a little better. I could see some of my shooting lanes and what the terrain was like. Of course, I couldn't see everything but forty five minutes later the sun rose and I could see everything much more clearly.

Looking back on this particular morning God began to show me something. He showed me that there are times in our lives that we wished that we could do more for someone. The truth is that even though we would want to do more, many times it would be very difficult to do or that person isn't ready or willing to allow us to help them. That's not to say we do nothing. John 8:12 says, "Then Jesus again spoke to them, saying, "I am the Light of the world; he who follows Me will not walk in the darkness, but will have the Light of life." (John 8:12, New American Standard Bible) As we ministered and prayed for people on the streets of L.A. I watched our team of 30 people bring a glimpse of light into the darkness they are living in. I saw people uplifted with a smile and someone building relationship with them. I saw hope restored. We experienced healing and watched God work in mighty ways. I saw the light of Jesus Christ shining into the lives of those who are stuck in the darkness of this world. It may have been a short moment as we passed through their life, but just like the morning the hunter passed by me in the darkness, we are believing they are beginning to see through that darkness and seeing all the blessings God has for them.

The truth is we should always be mindful of those around us and be ready and willing to speak into the lives of others. We should speak against the darkness of this world and speak life into their situations. The world is full of despair, depression, addiction, and so many other things that the devil uses to attack those around us. The good thing is, God almighty can and will defeat each and every attack. We just have to continue to stand with him and be willing vessels to be that light in the darkness. Now go make a difference in your world today!

Are you one that is willing to shine a light to others in their dark times?

Do you listen to what they are going through to see what it is they truly need?

PART OF THE PROCESS

About 10 years ago I purchased a 90 acre parcel of land adjacent to a wildlife management area. The deer are prevalent on the property and with good management we have seen an increase in shooter bucks over the years, but this wasn't my primary purpose for the property. I wanted to build a home and since the day I bought it I hoped I would someday do so. Not only did I want to build a home I also want to build a couple cabins on the property for couples who need time to reconnect or for pastors who just need time away. The property is overgrown due to it being logged a few years before I acquired the land which is great for being a safe place for deer to roam but not so great to build a home or the cabins. I've prayed for years to begin breaking ground with no movement towards our goal.

Recently I've been praying more often on what God has placed on our heart for this land and God really began to speak to me. For years I've prayed with expectation of God moving towards our goal. The problem was I was sitting still. God began to work on my heart and the Holy Spirit said to me, "If you're praying for it, then why haven't you been preparing for the blessing. Where is your faith that it will be provided? There is no salvation without repentance. There is no harvest until the ground is broken." This hit me like a ton of bricks and has really changed the way I look at things. Look at it this way. You aren't going to fill the freezer with venison until you decide to sight in your bow, get up and brave the elements, draw your bow back, focus, and let the arrow fly.

The truth is we have to become a participant in our blessings. We have to get up and do something. James 2:17 says, "In the same way, faith by itself, if it is not accompanied by action, is dead."(James 2:17, New International Version) I can have faith all day long that God will provide but if I don't get off my tail and prepare for the blessings I've prayed for, then how can God move on my part. This goes for all aspects of our life. If you're wanting a better job, then do the work needed for God to bless you with it. If you are wanting to become a world class archer, you have to put in the work to do so. Never expect blessings without you doing your part.

I encourage you today to start moving toward the things you've prayed about. Show God that the faith you have in Him is real. Don't be the person who 10 years from now says that they've been praying for something for years and they don't know why it hasn't happened yet. The reason it probably hasn't happened is because they haven't made one step towards the blessing God has waiting for them. They've expected God to do all the work. Pray about it, get up, move forward, prepare for what he has for you, and use your blessings to be a blessing to Him and others.

Is there something you've been praying or and it hasn't seemed to happen yet?

Have you done your part in the process or have you placed it all on God?

What is your next step in the process?

BLESSINGS IN DISGUISE

In 2005 I purchased the land that I hunt on. The property had never been managed well and the buck to doe ratio weighed heavily in the does' favor. For the first five years I saw doe after doe and hardly ever saw a buck. It got to the point that I was frustrated with the number of does in the area. I had seen groups with nearly 30 in a single group. I would harvest my does on the first day of each season and hunt hard for a buck without seeing any antlers at all. The hunters around my property weren't letting smaller bucks go to let them grow. That was part of the problem. The first five years I owned the property I saw only three bucks. This wasn't due to lack of effort. I hunted hard and often while the continuous flow of slick heads slipped by.

After the fifth year the buck population began to creep up on the doe numbers. I began to see more bucks, but they were small and young. We've let bucks go for three years now and next year we are looking to have some of the biggest bucks I've ever been close to. As I sat in the stand thinking about this during part of my tree stand therapy time, I realized that I was taking for granted the does I had on my property in the past. We have great numbers of deer in our area and if it weren't for the numbers, we have then we wouldn't be able to harvest as many animals as we do each year. Another thing I realized was with all those does in the past I was able to really work on many different things. I worked on scent control, my movement in the stand, stand location, and even patterning the bucks we have today. In fact, the does that I watched day after day were making me a better hunter. Once I realized this, I was thankful for all those slick heads.

Taking things for granted flows throughout most of our lives. We take our spouse for granted, our children, job, church, and even our friends. At times we become relaxed in our relationship with our Lord and Savior and even take God for granted. We don't realize or acknowledge those things that we need to be thankful for. Colossians 3:17 says, "And whatever you do, whether in word or deed, do it all in the name of the Lord Jesus, giving thanks to God the Father through him." (Colossians 3:17, New International Version) I've realized that even through the trials of life, I should give thanks to God. Through those trials God has been the teacher and is always helping me grow. I should always be grateful for those around me, the things I am blessed with, and every bit of oxygen I breathe.

Sometimes it takes some quiet time in a tree stand to see the big picture and how much all those small things really do mean. Most of the time those things you think are small are actually very big in your life. Take some time today to acknowledge the things that you're taking for granted. It could be your wife, kids, job, friends, or even God. Once your eyes are open give thanks to God and if some of those are people in your life, go tell them how thankful you are for them.

Are there things in life that you're not being appreciative that you should be?

How can you change your perspective to see the blessing in each of them?

NEEDS FOR GROWTH

As we all know the bucks are growing their antlers this time of year. I know for myself I can't wait to see the game cam pics as they seem to change daily. It's an exciting time of year for those who have a passion for deer hunting and for seeing bucks hit the potential they are genetically gifted with. It takes certain factors for a buck to become of a trophy caliber. Genetics is the top of the list. Bucks that come from a gene pool with large antler growth along with different characteristics will more than likely become a trophy. Other things that are key in allowing the genetic potential to show itself are age and nutrition. It takes time for a buck to grow into the animal he is capable of becoming. This is why selective harvest and letting bucks go to let them grow is key. Nutrition is another important factor in the process. A buck can have the best genetics out there but if he doesn't have the nutrients needed for antler growth he will never become what he was destined to become.

As I was sitting here dreaming about the growth of some the deer in our area, I began to see the parallel in our lives with the growth of a deer. For us to grow into the potential God has for us we need the same three things the deer has being genetics, age, and nutrition. As far as genetics when we turn our life over to Christ and allow the Holy Spirit to work in and through us when then have the perfect genetics inside each of us. There is nothing more perfect than the Holy Spirit. Romans 8:11 says, "But if the Spirit of Him who raised Jesus from the dead dwells in you, He who raised Christ Jesus from the dead will also give life to your mortal bodies through His Spirit who dwells in you." (Romans 8:11, New American Standard Bible)

Now that we have the first and most important part of the formula the next is age. When we become new in Christ it takes time to develop and to grow. We don't grow to our potential overnight and it takes patience to maneuver through life with the Father guiding us along the way. Galatians 5:25 says, "If we live by the Spirit, let us also walk by the Spirit."(Galatians 5:25, New King James Version) It takes learning of dangers and being aware of our surroundings constantly to be careful not to take a possible fatal step. The Holy Spirit shows us those things as we listen to Him and he teaches us along the way.

Lastly, we need nutrition through each step. Just as the buck needs good nutrition, and his nutrition comes from different things, we need the same. Our nutrition comes from many places. Some comes from reading of the Word and applying that to every area of our lives. It could come from prayer. It also comes from other believers speaking into our lives. We need all of these things to reach the potential God has for us.

The truth is God created each and every one of us for a purpose. That purpose is to grow His kingdom through the dreams, passions, and ideas God placed in our hearts. God has given you ideas, talents, passions, and dreams and wants you to step out in faith in Him to use those things for His glory. He has given you the genetics in the Holy Spirit as the foundation of your growth. He has given you life and time to grow in Him and develop into what he wants you to be. He has also given you the Word, prayer, and other believers to feed you along the way. I encourage you to make the decision today to do everything you can to reach the potential God has placed inside you. If you haven't given your life to Him I encourage you to do so today. If you have done that but haven't pursued Him, make that decision today to rededicate yourself to Him being the number one thing in your life. Trust me when I say that these are the best decisions anyone could ever make in their life.

Are you pursuing the things that are needed to reach your true potential in life?

Can you see what is needed daily to help reach that potential?

Can you see the importance of daily nutrition in reading the word, prayer, and having other to talk to and to ask question?

IT'S ALL ABOUT PERSPECTIVE

We've all seen the joy and the excitement in the eyes of a hunter when they've harvested an animal. It's undeniable that the joy is there and that it's overwhelming. I remember my kid's first successful hunt and the look in their eyes and the uncontrollable smile that covered their face. As a hunter, we've all experienced it ourselves.

A few years ago, I was hunting in New Mexico and was pursuing a mule deer that was well over 200 inches. The third day I found myself 200 yards away with nothing but grass and small brush between us. I began to crawl with my bow and after two and a half hours I made my way into 40 yards of the bedded buck with two does. The sun was beginning to disappear over the horizon and the last few rays of sun were causing the buck's antlers to shine over the grass he was bedded in. I realized that my time was running out and I had to make a decision. I could wait and hope he stood up before the light died, or I could make a move. I decided to draw my bow back and once I was at that point, I would whistle in hopes the buck stood up to see what was going on. As I started my draw one of the does stood up to stretch and caught me at half draw. I froze. She stared. I had one of two options. I could let my bow down or come to full draw. I decided to come to full draw and as I did the doe fled and the buck spun out of his bed to follow her. I quickly let an arrow fly.

As I watched the buck disappear over the ridge to my south I turned back to a friend of mine that was a half mile away watching the stalk unfold. I raised my hands in the air and was overwhelmed with joy. He hurried down to me in nearly a dead run and put his arms around me and explained how awesome it was to watch. He then said "Let's go get him". I looked back at him and informed him that I had missed. He looked at me in shock and began to ask why I through my hands in the air and why I was so excited. I simply told him that even though I had missed it was the most exciting hunt of my life and the joy of the opportunity just overtook me at that moment. In the time I sat and waited for my friend to get to me I knelt down on my knees and to be honest shed a few tears. Not because I missed but because God is such a good God and allowed me to be part of such an amazing experience.

You see, it's all about perspective. We can focus on failure and those storms that we walk through in life, or we can focus on God and what he is doing through that storm. Of course, life throws us curve balls and makes things difficult at times, but we can't allow our joy to be lost. What we should do is live a life that reflects James 1:2-3 which says, "Consider it all joy, my brethren, when you encounter various trials, knowing that the testing of your faith produces endurance."(James 1;2-3, New American Standard Bible) The truth is God isn't causing the struggle we are going through. He's not the one that puts us through pain and struggle. He is the one that is bringing us through it and makes us stronger as we walk through the storm. He is right there beside us and never leaves us and in that alone we should hold onto the joy he gives us.

I encourage you the next time you're going through a trial in your life to stop and check your perspective. Are you looking at the storm, or are you looking at God who is beside you in the storm? I can tell you that the perspective you are coming from will greatly affect how you come out of that storm. More than likely if you focus on the storm you will come out weak and weary, but if you focus on God you will come out stronger and more resilient. I've done both in the past and I know from experience that the only way is to look at God and allow him to walk you through it and protect you along the way.

What does success look like to you?

Do you find the success even when it looks like failure?

Are you one to find the good even when it looks bad?

LOST AND IN THE DARK

My hunting career started when I was 19 years old. Up to that point in my life I had squirrel hunted with my grandfather a few times and really enjoyed the experience. I had been given permission to hunt on a family friend's property on Turkey Creek. I had no idea what I was doing or what I was even looking for as I started to scout the area. I had never had a mentor to teach me the ways of hunting the elusive whitetail. As I ventured forth throughout the woods I started noticing trees that had been ripped to shreds in the area. I continued to follow this line of trees until I came to a curve in a creek where a heavily used trail was located. The tracks were many and going both directions up both steep embankments of the creek. This is where I decided to hunt and put all my eggs in one basket. The problem was I had no idea where I was at. This plot of land was large and after walking through cane breaks that seemed to reach to heaven, I wasn't quite sure how I had gotten to this point. I knew the general direction I needed to go but I didn't have a set path to be able to find this spot again. So I walked back to the west until I came to the creek that I had crossed and as I followed this creek I found the old fallen oak tree I had walked across to get to the other side. Once I got to that point, I had my bearings straight and had a pretty good idea of how to find that spot once opening day of rifle season arrived.

Opening day was finally upon us and I didn't go hunt that morning because I really wasn't positive I could walk in and locate my stand. I had talked my brother into going with me so that I wouldn't have to go alone. As we pulled to the back of the pasture where I would enter into the woods, my brother decided he was just going to hunt near the truck. I grabbed my rifle and my pack and headed deep into the woods, and after crossing the old dead tree I easily walked back to my stand location. I sat all evening and only saw a few deer and no bucks came within sight. Just before dark I was just about to get up and head back to the truck when I heard something rustle in the brush. As I sat and waited, daylight began to disappear and the moonless night had overtaken me. Equipped with a small flashlight I began to head back to the truck. Amid the confusion of all the cane thickets and every tree looking the same, I had ventured off my path and was headed in a southwestern direction rather than due west. A 20 minute walk had turned into 45 minutes at this point and I had finally run upon a creek. Was this the right creek or had I run upon one of the other creeks in the area? As I started walking down the creek, nothing looked familiar and the old oak bridge wasn't to be found. I walked to the left down the creek for a ways, and then back the other direction. I was at a point of fear and panic. I had never been in a situation like this before. With the pride I had in me, I didn't want to admit my failure to get back to the truck, but at this point I finally yelled for my brother.

Fortunately, he heard me and turned the headlights on in the truck. After an hour of aimlessly wandering in the dark I could see the faint glow of the lights through the timber. As I headed that direction and the truck drew closer and closer, the fear and anxiety had finally subsided, and I felt safe once again. This experience is reflective of our spiritual journey in this world. I gave my life to the Lord at the age of 31 and before that point I was aimlessly pursuing things of this world. I was in the dark without heavenly guidance and I was on the wrong path. I somewhat knew there had to be a God but I had never even been spoken to about who he really is. The things that were important in life at that point were money, money, and what I could get with money. I was focused on things of this world rather than having a heavenly mindset. It took the death of my best friend Gavin and his brother inviting me to church and praying for me constantly to finally open my eyes to the light through the dark forest. I didn't understand the death of Gavin at that time but over the years I have seen how God works even through the worst of tragedies. Through that experience his family drew closer to God. I gave my life to Christ. My kids have been saved along with many people that I have come in contact with over the years. Today I consistently focus on God and what he has for me. I actively seek his guidance in everything I do and I do my best to be a willing vessel for him to reach others.

If at this point in your life you haven't given your life to Christ, I urge you today to find someone to speak to. It takes an acceptance in your heart of who God is, who Jesus Christ is and that he was crucified for our sins as a living sacrifice and rose again on the third day. It also takes a repentance of sin and the willingness to live a life for Christ. Since I gave my life to Christ, I've had more joy and peace in my heart over the last few years than all the years before. Christ is my first! God is the head of my everything. God is the head of my wife and my children. He is the head of my ambitions and my number one goal on this earth. I urge you to make the Lord the same in your life.

Do you find yourself lost and want to find your way?

Do you know anyone to talk to about this?

What fears you the most about reaching out to someone?

DANGER IN THE GOBBLE

If you live in the country, or if you've spent any amount of time in nature, you've probably spent some time sitting out listening to the gift of nature God has blessed us with. I sit here now watching the sun set over the pond listening for the sound of an ol' gobbler in his roost in hopes of drawing close to him come sunrise. Strangely enough after thirty minutes of listening I hadn't heard a sound. Suddenly a pack of coyotes begin to sound off and immediately one shock gobbles in response to the howls. Soon after a hoot owl echoes through the trees and once again the gobbler blows up. The ol' tom nearly made it all evening without giving up his location, but with his quick response in haste of those around him he gave his position away.

As I sit watching the last glow of the sun drift over the horizon and the sound of bugs begin to overtake the calm I begin to think about the response of the tom. By the time I heard him it was dark and he was definitely nestled in his safe place for the night. If he would have stayed calm and quite, he wouldn't have given up his position. In doing so he has put himself in harms way come daylight.

The more I think about it the more I realize how we are a lot like that tom many times throughout our life. I know for me there have been times I wish I would have just stayed calm and kept my mouth shut. But as many of us have done I reacted quickly in response to something and before I knew it I said something I wish I wouldn't have said.

Proverbs 18:21 says, "Death and life are in the power of the tongue, and those who love it will eat its fruits"(Proverbs 18:21, New International Version). Most of the time when we speak or respond quickly to something, we fail to put much thought into what we are saying. We respond out of emotion and many times the words we release aren't well received. Truthfully when we respond in this manner they shouldn't be well received. Hopefully the person on the other side of the conversation is thinking more clearly but many times the same happens with the other party as well. As we all know this can escalate quickly and things go down hill from there.

Ecclesiastes 3:7 says there's "a time to be silent, and a time to speak"(Ecclesiastes 3:7, New International Version). One of those times we should keep silent is when we respond from our emotions and honestly feelings don't always represent the truth. It's best to discipline yourself and step back, take a breath, and possibly come back to it later.

I know many people struggle with this very issue. If this is you I encourage you to pray and ask God to empower you to know when to talk and when not to. Ask him to show you how to handle those situations and how to approach it in and loving way. I'll be praying for you as well. I hate to see my brothers and sisters put themselves in a tough situation due to something they wish they wouldn't have said. Don't be like that ol' tom I'll be pursuing in the morning who has put himself in a bad situation because he couldn't tame his tongue.

Do you tend to respond before you stop to think if it's the way to do so?

Have you ever hurt a relationship by responding in haste?

What can you do to heal that relationship?

RESPOND TO THE CALL

A few years ago I was turkey hunting in SE Oklahoma with a couple of friends. Hunting was slow and as the morning progressed our pace had slowed as well. The turkey had gobbled on the roost but once they hit the ground they became silent. Mid-morning we decided to take a break to eat a snack and lay out our game plan for the rest of the day. I laid my pack against a large rock, sat down, and leaned back to rest for a moment and suddenly the sound of gobble resonated through the valley. We looked at each other and I grabbed my pack and urged them to get up. They looked up at me and said they were thinking it was another hunter that we had seen earlier who had used a gobble call a couple times earlier. I was certain this wasn't a man made sound and I headed towards the sound on my own as they continued to rest. As I drew closer to where I heard the sound I caught a glimpse of the gobbler dusting on an old abandoned road. I crawled as close as I could and began to slowly run my striker across the face of my slate. The bird instantly looked up and exploded into a full strut. Needless to say a few moments later I was able to squeeze the trigger. The explosion dropped the bird in his tracks and at the same time woke my buddies up as they rested on the ridge above.

I look back on this story and laugh a little. Still to this day I give both of them a hard time over it. But as I sit here and reflect on that moment I can't help but think about how this relates to our spiritual life. We had hunted all morning and walked miles trying to find what we had been looking for when suddenly we heard the gobble in the valley below. I was certain it was the sound of a tom turkey, one friend thought it was another hunter, and the other said he thought it was a tom but didn't want to waste more energy chasing something that might not be real.

As men we can fall into these 3 categories when it comes to hearing God's call. We can be the one who thought he heard what God was saying but didn't move forward because he was fearful of failure. We could be the one that heard from God but convinced himself that it wasn't God. To be honest I've been in both of those men's shoes many times in my life. God has put things on my heart that I either allowed fear to paralyze me from moving forward or I just discounted what I heard and convinced myself that it wasn't God at all. I know that many of you out there have been in those same shoes yourself and I know that it may seem difficult to distinguish the voice of God at times.

I've learned over time that God's voice is a small still voice and to hear it and to recognize it we need to constantly be listening for it. We must stay in relationship with Him continually. I know for myself that I want to be like men of the Bible such as Abraham, Joseph, and Matthew and I could name many more who heard his voice and without fear took each step in faith that God was with them. I encourage you today to listen to our Father in heaven. If he is calling you to a relationship with him then repent and walk towards him. If he has placed dreams or ideas in your heart that will bless you and in turn bless the kingdom then without fear take that first difficult step knowing that He is faithful and will be with your every step of the way. As for myself, I will not let fear slow me down. I serve a mighty God and with Him all things are possible,

Are you one to discount the things you hear in the spirit?

How do you respond to that small still voice?

WHERE'S THE BLAME

Over the years I've seen this and done this myself many times. I either missed a deer with my gun or bow and immediately went to blame it on the weapon. I've said that my scope must have been off, or my sights must have gotten knocked off somehow. For many years it seemed like the first deer that walked in that I took a shot at with my now I missed. It wasn't until a few years ago that I finally realized that one was always nerves. The truth is the fault is never the weapon. The fault only lays on the one holding it. It was our responsibility to have the sights correct or to make sure we were ready when the opportunity came.

We honestly do this with people also. We blame this and that on someone else. We blame our reactions on whatever they did or what they said. If they didn't do what they did, we wouldn't react that way. Right? This started with Adam when he turned to blame Eve for his disobedience in the garden. He knew what God said and he was right there when the serpent spun his web of lies.

Matthew 7:3-5 says, "Why do you see the speck that is in your brother's eye, but do not notice the log that is in your own eye? Or how can you say to your brother, 'Let me take the speck out of your eye,' when there is the log in your own eye? You hypocrite, first take the log out of your own eye, and then you will see clearly to take the speck out of your brother's eye." (Matthew 7:3-5, English Standard Version) We all have our own issues, yet we fail to see those in situations because we are focused on the other persons issues. We are only responsible for our own reactions. No matter what is said or done to us, how we react will be the factor of what direction it goes from there. A reaction to an argument will determine if it goes towards resolution or a bigger fight.

This goes for things that hit us in the world as well. If we lose our job, do we react by standing on God's Word or do we sink into depression. If we become sick, do we stand, or do we fall? Our reaction determines the quality of the outcome.

Our reaction is the catalyst to action. Whether that action is good or bad it is up to us to take our thoughts and actions captive and make sure we steer those things in the right direction and take ownership of what happens from there. The responsibility and blame is on us not them.

Do you tend to take responsibility for your reaction to things that happen around you?

Ultimately, who is in control?

SURPRISE ATTACK

Years ago, we were hunting with a friend and he was staying in the woods well after dark in hopes of not spooking the buck he was hunting. We were at the truck waiting for his return when suddenly he came bursting out of the woods and he was headed to the truck in a hurry. He yelled for us to get in the truck and we all kind of looked at each other. He was a jokester so we didn't get in any hurry. As he made it to the truck, jumped in, and slammed the door he looked at us and just laughed.

We thought he was joking but later we found out he really was filled with fear. He had been walking back to the truck with no flashlight and he heard something behind him. As he walked faster it kept pace even up to his sprint back to the truck. Once made it to the truck he realized that thing that was chasing him was a piece of barbed wire that has got wrapped up in his shoe lace, causing him to drag it behind him.

Thinking of this story it makes me think of how many times in life we allow fear to overwhelm us and knock us down or make us run like my friend did. It could be heartache, or it could be life or death that brings fear into our lives. It could be bills, sickness, or anything that knocks us back. It could be expected or unexpected either way God is telling us that he has our back no matter what is on our tail. Matthew 6:34 says, " Therefore do not worry about tomorrow, for tomorrow will worry about itself. Each day has enough trouble of its own." (Matthew 6:34, New International Version) God has us in the palm of his hands as he wants us all to hear what Isaiah 35:4 which says "Say to those with fearful hearts, "Be strong, do not fear; your God will come, he will come with vengeance; with divine retribution he will come to save you."(Isaiah 6:34, New International Version)

Remember that when you face fear that God will come with a vengeance. It doesn't say that he will skip in. It says with a vengeance. That's powerful. It means with great force and I can think of no other force I want fighting for me.

Has something came into your life that left you full of fear
or worry?

Did you handle it well?

How could you have handled it better?

CONFIDENCE IN THE LEADER

Years ago, I remember going to the woods for the first time in hopes of killing a deer. My dad decided it was time to take me hunting and we gathered everything we needed and headed out the door. We made it to the woods and settled in. Dad showed me how to load the gun and the began to call and teach me the ins and outs of hunting deer. I felt firmly confident that at any moment I would have the opportunity to pull the trigger even though that morning we saw nothing. If it were in my own knowledge, I would have been less confident and the only thing I would have grabbed was the rifle and probably would have never gotten the rifle loaded. It was having my dad there guiding me along the way that gave me hope and faith that good things were ahead of us. If had been alone I more than likely would have felt lost and confused.

This came to mind yesterday as I was driving down Main Street here in the town I live. As we were approaching the red light, I noticed a young girl in a wheel chair. She was cruising down Main Street swerving side to side and spinning whenever she had a chance. She was full of joy and confidence right where she was. What I noticed next was that about 10 feet ahead of her was father and it hit me. Her confidence came from knowing that her father was leading the way and opening the doors on the path she was traveling.

In both of these situations, we were being led by our earthly fathers which brought joy and confidence. The thing is that joy and confidence in those situations are only a slight taste of the joy and confidence that we experience when we are following our Heavenly Father. Authentic joy and true happiness is only found in His presence. 1 Chronicles 16:27 says "strength and joy fill his dwelling" (1 Chronicles 16:27, New Living Translation). Another thing that hit me as I began to ponder these two events is that joy is ever present in and through every season when our focus is in the Lord. This even goes for those times of struggle. What we have to do in those times is to trust God and the future he promises us.

I want to encourage you today to choose joy. No matter the situation and no matter the struggle, the true essence of joy that comes from focusing on God will pull you through. This can't be confused with happiness that is only an emotion. Joy comes from knowing who you are, why you are, how you are and most of who you belong to. In the knowing of these things joy will begin to take over the way you live your life.

Do you look at being joyful in all things?

Do you tend to look at the negative or the positive in most situations?

Is there an area you can focus on now?

WHAT IS GREATNESS

Have you ever sat back and thought what it would be like to reach a level of greatness? We tend to look all around us and see people that we consider great. Many times, we think of an athlete, a celebrity, or even a pastor. I mean they are great at what they do, right? For years I looked at the quarterback for the Green Bay Packers, Brett Favre, and thought that he was one of the greatest. Once I got over the love of football, I began to look up to people like Kevin Van Dam when I fished and Bill Jordan when I became focused on hunting. They were absolutely great at what the do.

The thing is, quite often as we focus on how great other people and in turn, we fail to realize the greatness in ourselves. We discount the value that we have. We look at these great hunters that kill record book bucks year after year and think, "Why can't I be like that?". We think to ourselves that we just aren't that good. The truth is you probably don't have the same opportunities that they do. This goes for many areas of our lives as well. We begin to think we aren't destined for greatness at all.

I want to tell you a secret that shouldn't be a secret at all. YOU ARE DESTINED FOR GREATNESS! Recently I began to take a look at what greatness is truly about. I began to look at people around myself and I took a look at my wife. Recently she has put her feet to the ground in an effort to reach out to the homeless in our community. Weekly she is going out and taking burritos and bags with necessary hygiene items to hand out as a way to build relationships and hopefully give opportunity to spread the gospel. I looked at my daughter who seven months ago gave birth to my first grandson. I look at the gift she has of being a mother and she has a heart of gold. I look back at my grandpa and remember how he was always gentle and always willing to teach me something that he was doing.

You see the world has put its own spin on what greatness looks like. It's become a status of importance, wealth, and influence. I would tend to say that the true definition of greatness is, "selflessly serving those around us for God's glory." So in saying that, greatness is inside each and every one of us. You can be great in the hunting industry. Take your grandchild out to enjoy God's gift of nature. Help a wounded warrior kill his first buck. Celebrate your wife's victory of killing the buck you've been after for years. Become great in your place of work by teaching someone below you the ropes and listening to their ideas. You might just help them advance beyond your level and that would be greatness in itself. Become someone's mentor and speak life into them daily.

Galatians 2:20 says, "I have been crucified with Christ: it no longer I who live, but Chrst lives in me; and the life which I now love in the flesh I live by faigh in the Son of God, who loved me and gave Himself for me." (Galatians 2:20, New King James Version) Christ gave himself for us and in our desire to be a reflection of him we should be willing to give yourself for those around us. That is what greatness is really about. So I challenge you today to walk daily in the greatness that is flowing inside of you. Don't allow it to stay inside but let it flow freely to those around you.

What do you consider to be greatness?

Can you see the greatness in you?

Can you see that the greatness is already there?

WHERE'S YOUR FOCUS

When I first decided to take up archery, I had no idea where to start. I went and purchased a bow and a dozen arrows. I then looked into releases and broadheads. As I began to shoot and to sight my bow in I became frustrated with myself as I continued to shoot. I would shoot for hours at a time and would never be happy with the groupings I was shooting. I would sometimes shoot all twelve arrows, and most would be in a group of three inches but then a few would be scattered further out. I became obsessed with placing all 12 arrows in a three inch circle and though many would be in that circle I was never pleased with what I was accomplishing.

One afternoon I was down to my last arrow of twelve and as I focused on the target, I slowly squeezed the release and the arrow hit the mark. I had finally placed all twelve arrows in a three inch circle!!! I was on a high and I immediately wanted to do it again. The first arrow of the next group missed it by a quarter of an inch. I immediately went from a high to frustration. About that time my friend showed up and asked how I was doing. I responded to him that I had just placed all twelve arrows in the circle, and he asked why I didn't seem excited about it. I told him that the very next arrow missed the mark by a quarter of an inch. He asked me why I had taken up the sport of archery. I explained I wanted to take a deer with my bow. Then he said something that made me open my eyes to the truth of the matter. He said, "If you focus on being perfect, you're never going to enjoy it. So if you can't enjoy it then why do it?"

It took me some time to realized that the mindset that I needed to be perfect was overtaking the joy I should have been receiving from shooting my bow. I had become consumed with perfection. This same thing creeps into our new life in Christ. I see many people when they fail after salvation become frustrated and lose the joy they should have. They become consumed with perfection and if they falter a slight bit it overtakes that joy. They sometimes continue to look at what they were before and begin to think that those things of their past will destroy them. Romans 3:22-24 says, "This righteousness from God comes through faith in Jesus Christ to all who believe. There is no difference, for all have sinned and fall short of the glory of God, and are justified freely by his grace through the redemption that came by Christ Jesus." (Romans 3:22-24, New King James Version) Jesus died for our sins and we have to completely understand and receive that. We all fail, and even though we all do our best to live a life that reflects the perfection of Jesus we will still falter at times in life. What we need to do is immediately see our failures and repent and give it to God. When I say truly give it to God that means turn it over to him and let it go. God forgives us and we need to do as he has done and forgive ourselves also.

Don't beat yourself up. Understand you aren't perfect. There was only one perfect one and that was Jesus. Allow the joy of the Lord to overtake your life. Enjoy the life you've been given. Do your best to reflect Christ. God doesn't expect perfection, or he wouldn't have given his son on the cross to cover your sins. If he doesn't expect perfection in you then you shouldn't either.

Do you focus on perfection rather than progression?

Do you allow the perfection mindset get in the way of the joy you could be experiencing?

WHERE'S THE PASSION

Over the years I have gained a great passion for the outdoors. I'm not sure if it started with the first tug of a fish on the end of my fishing line or the first time I encountered a whitetail as I was perched in a tree. I can say one thing though. I became consumed with the pursuit of whatever it was that I was chasing.

In my younger years I fished continually. At one point I fished 3 different bass tournament trails and would fish up to 300 days a year. If I wasn't fishing a tournament, I would be pre-fishing for one or scouting different areas of lakes I would fish in the future. Of course, when I had kids that slowed down considerably. Some time after that I became much more interested in hunting. Whether it be chasing a whitetail, turkey, elk, ducks, or even a hog, my passion grew more and more as time went on. I became completely immersed in the pursuit of the game I was seeking. Honestly my enthusiasm for hunting was extremely high and anyone that knows me could vouch for that.

In saying that, enthusiasm and passion are great to have, but as we become more caught up in what it is we are doing it can become detrimental at times. I realized this one evening as I was sitting in my tree stand. I had been tirelessly pursuing a buck that would score around 150 inches. It would be the biggest archery buck I've harvested if he would just show his face. As time passed slowly and as I looked intensely into the distance, I heard a gun shot. This worried me because it came from the direction the buck always traveled from. Time passed and I received a message on my phone that the buck had been shot from the road. A friend of mine was hunting across the road and had seen a truck pull up, shoot, and eventually drag the buck to his truck and take off. I was broken at that point. I had put hours and hours into chasing and patterning this deer. I honestly didn't have another deer that I was willing to shoot on our property and felt like not hunting any more that year. As I sat and I was feeling sorry for myself God began to speak to me. He placed a question in my heart at that moment that changed my life forever. He asked, "What if you pursued Me and my kingdom as passionately as you did the buck that you've been after?" As I sat there in the quiet and the stillness a tear rolled down my cheek. I realized at that moment that my pursuit of a deer had overshadowed my pursuit of God himself.

After I climbed down from the tree that evening the buck I had been chasing had nearly left my thoughts. God ministered to me for nearly an hour that evening as I sat and listened to what he began to download in my heart. A seed was planted that day that has done nothing but grow each day since that moment. My passion for God has grown and flourished as I've allowed him to provide the nourishment through the Word, fellowship with others, and the Holy Spirit. My enthusiasm for God, his kingdom, and his people that He sent Jesus to die for has and continues to grow daily. I recently found out the Greek meaning for the word enthusiasm. The root of enthusiasm is theos which means God and enthous means possessed by God, and inspired. I want to be a man that is possessed by God and inspired by his love and his word.

I want to take the question that God asked me that night and expand that a bit. "What if we all pursued God and his kingdom as passionately and enthusiastically as we do the worldly passions that we chase continually?" It could be a deer, bass, elk, a sport, hobbies, or anything that we gain a strong passion for. Have we become enthusiastic towards something of this world to the point that we have made it a God in our life and in turn placed it above the God that loves us and sent his son to die for us? I encourage you to stop and take a look at things in your life and honestly ask yourself if you've placed other things above God. Take an inventory of your time, thoughts, and your actions. Are they geared towards God even in the things that you are passionate about? Are you glorifying God in those things? If we all began to pursue God, the way we sometimes pursue things of this world we can then make a huge difference in the lives of those around us and in turn build his kingdom tremendously. If you are with me and want to give it all to God and have the greatest passion and enthusiasm for his kingdom, then shout a big Amen and focus daily on growing in him!

Do you tend to allow things of this world to overtake the need for God?

What seems to take priority as you go through life?

In what order to prioritize things and how do you need to realign those thing?

PUBLIC LAND WOES

The morning is still as I ease into the timber in hopes of hearing the sweet sound of an ol' gobbler as he sounds off for the first time of the morning. The air is crisp and the blanket of fog fills the air. Step by step I quietly maneuver down the trail and slowly make my way through the woods. I've anticipated this day for the last year. As I draw near to my destination I stop, close my eyes, say a quick prayer, and focus my attention to the sounds around me. A rooster sounds off in the distance. A coyote yelps across the valley. Then suddenly 50 yards to my left the sound of that ol' tom gets my heart racing.

I slowly ease back between a couple cedars and wait for the sun to begin to shine. It seemed like an eternity for the sun to rise that morning, but as it began to spread light across the countryside, I found the bird roosted high in the limbs of a large oak tree. The silhouette was beautiful against the rising glow of the sky. It was evident the bird I was pursuing was a mature tom with a thick, flowing beard. He began to sound off more frequently and my heart pounded harder with every gobble. I just knew this was going to be the best opening day ever.

Suddenly, I hear something to my left and as I glance that direction, I see another hunter almost running down the trail in my direction. I wave my arms back and forth as the tom is gobbling his head off and the the hunter stops and says out loud, "Oh, I'm sorry. I didn't see you." and headed back the other direction making just as much noise going as he did coming. The bird shut up and never made another sound and stayed in the tree for a half hour longer than he should have. As I saw him begin to spread out his wings, I realized he was going away from my direction.

Frustrated is a very good description of how I felt that morning. Of course, this is what you deal with when you hunt public land. As I made my way back to my truck, I became more frustrated when I see four trucks parked beside mine at the trail head. I've always been one to park at a trail head so that people know the direction I've more than likely gone. Especially while turkey hunting. I've also always been one who goes on to the next trail or a different area if someone is already in a certain area so that we aren't chasing after the same roosted gobbler.

As I loaded my gear, crawled in my truck, and started the engine I sat back and took a deep breath. As I prayed for peace in the situation the words of Jesus seemed to sound off in my ear saying, "Forgive them, for they know not what they do"(Luke 23:34, English Standard Version). Suddenly a peace came over me and I realized that even though I was frustrated in that situation, the other parties had no ill will in their actions. They were merely chasing after something and were focused fully on the purpose they were there for.

The truth is, more often than not when we become frustrated with other individuals their intentions were never meant to frustrate or hurt us. Most of the time they are merely focused on their individual life or what they were working towards and in doing so could possibly have not noticed how they could have done us wrong. We can always take a couple different courses of action in those situations. We can choose to get upset and allow the actions of the other person to ruin our day. We could also stop and realize that they more than likely never meant to harm us in any way at all. In most cases they never even realize what they have done.

I encourage you today to take a deep breath when you begin to become frustrated with someone around you. Think about it for a moment and ask yourself if you truly feel they were intentional in their actions towards you. Most likely they were not. Then take the words of Jesus on the cross to heart. "Forgive them, for they know not what they do." (Luke 23:34, English Standard Version)

Do you tend to let others affect you in a negative way?

Do you give others the benefit of the doubt?

How can you change your mindset on this matter?

PHARISEES OF THE HUNTING WORLD

Over the years I've become someone that loves to study and grow in my abilities as a hunter. I read articles and different studies on whitetail deer and how different people manage their properties. One thing I've noticed is how often people become confrontational over others methods. I've seen arguments over using modern muzzleloaders rather than the older traditional styles. I've seen people get in heated debates over using compound bows compared to recurves. One of the most argued point is the baiting of deer even where it's legal to do so. This is something that does nothing but hurt our legacy as outdoorsmen. We need to stand together in our sport and when people are hunting legally, we need to stand beside each other rather than condemn others for something that we may or may not practice.

We see this same thing throughout the Bible. The Pharisees, or the religious leaders, were some of the worst. In Mark 3:1-6 Jesus was in the synagogue and noticed a man with a deformed hand. The Pharisees were watching closely to see what Jesus would do and if he healed the man they were going to accuse him or working on the Sabbath. Jesus turned to them after asking the man to come to him and asked, "Does the law permit good deeds on the Sabbath, or is it a day for doing evil? Is this a day to save life or destroy it?"(Mark 3:4, New International Version) There was no answer from the Pharisees. Jesus was saddened by the hardened hearts of the religious leaders then healed the man. Immediately the Pharisees went and met with the supporters of Herod and plotted how to kill Jesus.

These were men that believed in God but were so stubborn in their ways that it got in the way of their walk. They were self-righteous and believed that their way was the only way and those who didn't do things their way, were wrong, including God himself in Jesus. We can get in this same state of mind if we begin to become self-righteous ourselves. I truly believe if all the denominations would stop arguing about the very small percentage of things they don't agree on and focus on the large percentage of what they do agree on, then this world could be changed.

If today you see yourself beginning to think self-righteously in your walk with God or even in the way you hunt, then take a step back and see that there may be other ways to go about the same love that we all have. Stand together for Christ and never look at your way as being the only way to make disciples. Stand beside those of other denominations and work together in the 95% you agree on and never let the 5% get in the way. Also stand beside other outdoorsmen and help our legacy as hunters, fishermen, and outdoorsmen grow and withstand the test of time. Unity is a powerful thing!!!

Do you find yourself judging others for doing things differently than you?

How can you stop yourself from doing so?

Is there something in your heart you need to deal with now?

BE STILL AND LISTEN

I remember the first time I ever pursued a turkey. I went with a friend of mine who had chased them for years. The cool air of the morning was crisp, and it seemed like nothing was rustling across the valley. As the slight glow of the sun began to silhouette the limbs of the trees my friend blasted the sound of an owl through the leaves. He turned to me and and said "Be still and listen." Suddenly in the distance we heard the faint sound of a gobbler responding. We made our way his direction and would stop ever so often and be still and listened to locate him. We finally made it close to where he was perched in the limbs of an old oak tree and set up. Unfortunately, he was much more interested in the hens that were clucking on the other side of him, but there was something that stuck with me over the years and that was what my friend said that morning as we first started that morning. That sentence was. "Be still and listen."

Over the years that short sentence has probably made one of the biggest impacts on my life. When it comes to my wife, I've learned that we need time together to slow down and talk about God, currently life situations, and the future. It showed me that it's extremely important to use the ears God has given me to listen to what she has to say and to what God has placed on her heart rather than to always have to be heard. With my kids it's taught me that stepping back from our busy lives and taking time to spend time and listen to them makes for a much better relationship. In our workplaces and our relationships with our friends it's just as important to stop and listen to those around us.

Of course, the biggest impact is when I learned that I have to be still and listen to what God has to say. So many times in life we begin to pray to God to unload all our burdens, struggles, and wants to him but we fail to stop and listen to what He has to say. Prayer is a two-way conversation and many times we fail to receive the direction that God is trying to give us. We become to become engulfed in what we want in life or the stumbling blocks along the way and we fail to stop and listen our Father in heaven. It's funny that when we are chasing an ol' gobbler we call and we take time afterwards to hear his response, but when we are talking to God many times we call out to Him but don't stop to listen to what He has to say. It's imperative that we allow pray to be that two-way conversation.

I encourage you today to first make sure you take time to pray and talk to God. I also encourage you to make sure to stop and listen to what He has to say. It's the most important part of that conversation and many times the key to a better life.

Do you usually just tell God what you want and don't take the time to have that two-way conversation.

Do you take time to have the same commitment to those in your life?

Do you tend to only focus on what's on your mind rather than what others have to say?

SURPRISE, SURPRISE

Many years ago, I hunted with a few older men in southeast Oklahoma. These men were as ornery as anyone I've ever known. There were pranks and jokes flying around all the time, but when it came to hunting they were serious. They were territorial and didn't like others treading on their ground. The pack leader was named Buck and you never knew when to trust him unless he was hunting, and he never messed around much when it came to that.

Season had been slow and the last day of rifle season had rolled around and we were all hunting the same piece of property when we heard a gunshot. As always, everyone gave it about an hour and then we all would head that direction to see if any assistance was needed. As I walked up to the group Buck was telling them about the size of the deer he had shot. Needless to say,everyone was ready to trail the deer. He pointed out the first spot of blood and some hair and we all turned into blood hounds. The blood was plentiful for about 30 yards, and then it was like a needle in a haystack for the next hour. I was the young one of the group and was the one crawling looking for specks of blood.

After nearly an hour and a half of searching we were just about to give up when I found what I had been working so hard for. Well it wasn't exactly what I thought I was looking for. Buck had shot a squirrel and walked as far as he could, making a blood trail along the way and then hid the squirrel under the leaves. When I saw the tail sticking out I realized that I had been had by a bunch of old tricksters and had wasted my entire morning hunt.

As I sat and thought about the experience, I realized we do the same thing many times throughout our lives. We go out searching for things of this world that we think are going to be amazing and will fill a void. We go out chasing fame, fortune, relationships, and so many other things but in the end, we realize that wasn't what we were really looking for. We just knew that something was missing. In my past I worked extremely hard for some of the same things but came to a point that the void that was in my life wasn't something. It was someone and that someone was Jesus Christ. Colossians 3:2 says, "Set your mind on the things that are above, not on things that are on the earth." (Colossians 3;2, English Standard Version) When you truly turn your mind and your actions toward God your perspective on the things of this world are put into order. You gain a peace about yourself that you have never experienced before. The things you focus on are changed and your mind is made anew and redirected. Joy begins to fill your heart and begins to spread to others. As Phil Robertson would say, it makes you "Happy, Happy, Happy!!"

I know from experience that God changed my attitude toward life and changed my way of thinking. Yes there are times that I still fail but I'm quickly redirected to the path God has for me. If today you feel the world is getting in the way of your relationship with God, and if it's affecting the way you feel or act, take a moment to say a prayer and ask God to redirect your thoughts. Ask him to help realign your mind and your actions with his. God has great plans for each of us and when we allow him to lead we won't end up chasing down a squirrel that's blown to pieces.

Has life given you exactly what you've been looking for?

Has life surprised you at times?

How did you handle those moments?

CAMOFLAUGE ISN'T ALWAYS THE BEST

Many years ago I was hunting on the opening weekend of black powder season here in Oklahoma. At this point in my hunting career I hadn't started using tree stands so I was nestled back against an old oak in a line of trees connecting two large stands of timber. As the morning ticked away, I had become a little restless and bored to say the least. As I scanned the tree line, I noticed a squirrel about 40 yards from me scampering from tree to tree. Of course, this was the same squirrel that had my adrenaline flowing numerous times throughout the morning as he sounded like a 200 inch buck walking through the leaves. I decided to see if I could call this squirrel closer to me, so I slid my arms inside my jacket and ran my hand up to my cheek. I had always been able to make the sound of a squirrel barking by pulling air into my cheeks and using my hand to tap my cheek forcing the air out to make the sound. I made the first call to the squirrel and he took notice immediately and started intensely trying to find where the sound came from. Once again, I called out to him and the squirrel began to hop my way closing the distance to 10 yards. I was completely camouflaged and as I made the bark sound again, he rushed over and was sitting only 2 inches from the end of my barrel that was laid over my lap. I decided that I needed to scare the squirrel off just in case I needed to move to get a shot on a deer he wouldn't jump and cause the deer to flee. So I made a big movement towards the squirrel and rather than him bounding off he decided to use my head for a spring board to get in the closest tree possible. Of course, I rolled away thinking the evil varmint was about to tear me up in turn causing any deer that could be in the area to scatter. Afterwards I found it very funny and a time I will never forget.

When I was thinking about this moment from my past I realized that I was so camouflaged that the squirrel couldn't see me. This got me to thinking, "Can we sometimes become too camouflaged?" As we go throughout our life we sometimes try to blend into the crowd so that we don't have to feel different. The truth is, as Christians we need to seem different to the world that is lost so that they can see Christ in us. Matthew 5:14-16 (NIV) says, "You are the light of the world. A town built on a hill cannot be hidden. Neither do people light a lamp and put it under a bowl. Instead they put it on its stand, and it gives light to everyone in the house. In the same way, let your light shine before others, that they may see your good deeds and glorify your Father in heaven." (Matthew5:14-26, New International Version) So stop trying to blend into all of your surroundings. Camouflage is great in a deer stand or hunting from the ground but in our daily walk the camouflage doesn't help the light shine to the rest of the world. Take the camo off and let Jesus shine through.

Do you find yourself just trying to fit in?

How can you stand out for God?

THE SEASON TO COME

The last day of deer season has passed. The rain and fog filled every moment as I sat quietly in the blind. For two hours the cardinals, woodpeckers, and sparrows were the only things moving. Suddenly a group of hogs moved in and I released an arrow and took down a big sow. Of course, I heard the noise I was hoping it was a deer. As the darkness was overtaking the daylight my opportunity to harvest one more deer was quickly fading away. Suddenly I look to my right and a doe and a yearling were making their way in. I eased my bow up and as I came to full draw, I realized the darkness had consumed all the light I needed to take a shot. My pins were dark and I couldn't find the deer in my peep. The season was over.

As I had walked out of the woods I had begun to reflect upon this season. It looked extremely promising early with numerous nice bucks showing up on camera. Several times the deer showed up just as I was out of shooting light. Other times I would be in one stand and a shooter would show his face at a different stand. I harvested three does along the way but could never close the deal on a buck. My wife harvested a doe and one of my boys harvested a young buck.

Overall the season was still good to us putting meat in the freezer for the coming year. Of course, it would have been nice to harvest a buck or the doe that came in minutes after the season had expired.

In my time of reflection, I began to think of the seasons that were approaching. Of course, deer season is over but now is a time for us to try to eliminate the hog population that destroyed much of our deer season. At the same time, we will be shed hunting with turkey season following closely behind that. The summer will be filled with fishing and scouting for deer. Once again deer season will come. With each season bringing great expectation and excitement. We never know what is in store for us, but the hope and anticipation is what keeps us going.

As I think about this, I can't help but see the parallel to the seasons we go through in our everyday life. Seasons come and seasons go. Sometimes we are excited and at times we move forward with uncertainty. The one thing we can always be certain of is that God will be there. Hebrews 13:8 says, "Jesus Christ is the same yesterday and today and forever." (Hebrews 13;8, New International Version) Being that forever is for every season that is ahead of us we can always move forward with hope and anticipation of what God can and will do in our lives. We just need to trust him and allow our faith to strengthen us along the way.

So, if you're seasons are changing and you've become uncertain and nervous about what's ahead, I want to encourage you to see the greatness of God in your life. Know that God is with you every step of the way and you have the best father a person could have. He will not let you down. He will not abandon you. He will not leave you without. He loves you with a love that is forever etched in stone. Walk forward with hope and great anticipation of what God has in store for you.

Do you worry, or do you look at the next season of life with great anticipation?

What worries you most about what is to come?

TO AND FROM

I was sitting around this morning thinking about the first few years I hunted. As I was doing this, one particular event came to mind. I was excited and nervous to get out in the field that morning. I was young and didn't know much at all. I had scouted the land I was blessed to hunt for a couple of weeks and had found some signs of deer in the area. That morning I waited until daylight to head to where I was going to hunt because I wasn't sure of my mental compass. I arrived just as the sun appeared over the horizon and I draped the gun sling over my shoulder and began to rush in the timber. I had my head down and I was on a mission to get set up for the morning when I suddenly heard a loud blow and the brush explode just feet away. I looked up and a huge buck was tearing through the brush leaving the area that I was planning to sit. Needless to say I never saw that buck again and that morning I didn't see another deer. I actually only saw one other deer that year and wasn't able to even get a shot off.

As I was looking back at this occurrence, I was thinking that if I had only been hunting and been seeking every step of the way, I might have harvested a nice buck. I may not have missed that opportunity.

I did learn from that experience and ever since that day I always hunt to and from my stand. This is the same principle I carry in my everyday life when it comes to the Lord. When I was new in Christ, I was on fire for him through the church service and as I was walking out the doors of the church. That fire seemed to burn less and less the further away I walked and by the time the next day arrived I let the world take over again. Throughout the week I failed to look toward God and looked at my own abilities to solve my problems. The next week that same thing would happen on Sunday. I would catch fire and it would slowly fizzle out as Monday and Tuesday rolled around.

The good news is the more times I caught fire the longer the fire burned. I began to seek God throughout the week and apply him to all situations. Psalm 105:4 says, "Search for the Lord and for his strength; continually seek him." (Psalm 105:4, New Living Translation) We must seek God everyday and apply him to every hour and every minute of our life. When God revealed this to me it completely changed my life. Those things that I struggled with on a day-to-day basis were slowly being erased. The worry, stress, and anger were being washed away. I began to find peace and joy, even in those times of struggle. I began to see opportunities that I had been missing. Before, my mind was on what I could get done and how I could handle things. Now I give it all to God because he wants good for me.

Do you find yourself in this same cycle of bursts of fire and then in fire fades? Do you let the world take over as soon as you leave the church? It doesn't have to be that way. God wants you to know that he is there 24/7 and that your fire can continually burn. Deuteronomy 4:29 says, "But if from there you seek the Lord your God, you will find him if you seek him with all your heart and with all your soul." (Deuteronomy 4:29, New International Version) It doesn't matter where you are. If you seek him you will find him. You can be in one of your darkest moments and if you turn and seek him you will find the light. Make a conscious effort today to seek him every step of the day. Allow him to keep your fire lit so that you won't get lost in the dark.

Do you find your fire fizzling out the further you walk away from the church?

How can you change that?

NEVER SELL YOURSELF SHORT

Have you ever seemed to be wandering aimlessly in life? For years I was that way in pretty much every possible way. In my career I was just going through the motions day by day. In my relationships I would wake up and go with the flow and whatever happened, happened. In my time in the woods I would just climb a tree in the middle of nowhere in hopes something would come my way. I was walking around with the mindset that God placed me here to bless me. That's what the scripture says right? "May he give you the desire of your heart and make all your plans succeed. (Psalm 20:4,: New International Version). For years I focused on the first part of this scripture and quoted it often. I would tell people that if it's God's will then it will work out. What I was failing to do is to notice the second half of that scripture. It says "and make all your plans succeed". Now wait, you mean that I have to make plans to achieve the desires of my heart? It wasn't until I began to focus on the second part of that scripture that my life began to become more successful.

So what are plans? Plans are nothing more than a path towards a goal and a man without a plan is like an arrow without fletchings. It's very difficult to hit the goal you are shooting for. To go even deeper into that, a man without a goal is a man without direction in life. If you don't have something to shoot for then what exactly are you doing? The thing is if I had never set a goal at all, I probably wouldn't have reached much success at all.

In 2018 I have set a few goals for myself and for this ministry. I have learned to set the bar high. I do this because we can always go further than we realize we can. In doing that we sometimes fail to achieve the goal we have set and in all actuality we should never hit the mark 100% of the time. Why is that? If that were the case, then we are setting the mark to low and it will make us complacent in doing only what we feel we can do in our flesh. We begin to place ourselves as the only factor into reaching our mark and we fail to allow God to help us along the way. You see in moving forward we can only go so far on our own but with the help of the Holy Spirit we can go so much further.

I want to encourage you to set goals for the coming year. I also want you to share those goals with others that can hold you accountable. Set out a plan to reach those goals. Pray about it. Vocally speak out your goals in prayer to the Lord. Write them down and place them where you can see them daily. Begin to take steps in the direction of those goals. At the end of this year if you do these things, I promise you will have achieved or come much closer to the goals you set today. Now get moving.

Are you one to set goals?

Do you set goals easy to accomplish?

Do you set goals that push the limits?